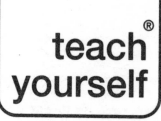

teach yourself

beginner's russian script
daphne west

D1222781

For over 60 years, more than 40 million people have learnt over 750 subjects the **teach yourself** way, with impressive results.

be where you want to be
with **teach yourself**

The author would like to thank Elena Kelly and Tracy Walsh for their help in the preparation of this book and Tatyana Izmailova for her constant support.

For UK order enquiries: please contact Bookpoint Ltd, 130 Milton Park, Abingdon, Oxon OX14 4SB. Telephone: +44 (0) 1235 827720. Fax: +44 (0) 1235 400454. Lines are open 09.00–18.00, Monday to Saturday, with a 24-hour message answering service. Details about our titles and how to order are available at www.teachyourself.co.uk

For USA order enquiries: please contact McGraw-Hill Customer Services, PO Box 545, Blacklick, OH 43004-0545, USA. Telephone: 1-800-722-4726. Fax: 1-614-755-5645.

For Canada order enquiries: please contact McGraw-Hill Ryerson Ltd, 300 Water St, Whitby, Ontario L1N 9B6, Canada. Telephone: 905 430 5000. Fax: 905 430 5020.

Long renowned as the authoritative source for self-guided learning – with more than 40 million copies sold worldwide – the **teach yourself** series includes over 300 titles in the fields of languages, crafts, hobbies, business, computing and education.

British Library Cataloguing in Publication Data: a catalogue record for this title is available from the British Library.

Library of Congress Catalog Card Number: on file.

First published in UK 2000 by Hodder Arnold, 338 Euston Road, London, NW1 3BH.

First published in US 2000 by Contemporary Books, a Division of the McGraw-Hill Companies, 1 Prudential Plaza, 130 East Randolph Street, Chicago, IL 60601 USA.

This edition published 2003.

The **teach yourself** name is a registered trade mark of Hodder Headline Ltd.

Copyright © 2000, 2003 Daphne West

Typeset by Transet Limited, Coventry, England.
Printed in Great Britain for Hodder Arnold, a division of Hodder Headline, 338 Euston Road, London NW1 3BH, by Cox & Wyman Ltd, Reading, Berkshire.

Hodder Headline's policy is to use papers that are natural, renewable and recyclable products and made from wood grown in sustainable forests. The logging and manufacturing processes are expected to conform to the environmental regulations of the country of origin.

Impression number   10 9 8 7 6
Year   2009 2008 2007 2006 2005

contents

Teach Yourself Beginner's Russian Script is the course to use if you are a complete beginner who wants to learn the Russian alphabet, or if your knowledge of Russian has become rusty and you need to refamiliarize yourself with the alphabet. The purpose of this book is to present the letters gradually, giving lots of practice and revision sections, so that by the end of the course you will feel able to read and to write Russian script. This course will get you started and give you the confidence to move on to study other aspects (listening, speaking, grammar).

Russian script – how 'different' is it?

The complete beginner can sometimes feel that Russian might be rather difficult to learn because the script, initially, looks very different. Russian is from the same 'family' of languages as English (Indo-European) and has been very much influenced by languages such as Latin and French, but also by Greek, Hebrew and Old Church Slavonic. In the 9th century a monk called St Cyril is reputed to have devised the Russian script – hence its name: *Cyrillic*. It is possible to transliterate Russian words (i.e. produce an approximation of their sound by using English letters), but this can be very time consuming – sometimes we need as many as four English letters to produce the sound of one Russian letter. Thanks to St Cyril there are only 33 letters in the Russian alphabet and it is made up of the same sort of components as the English alphabet (consonants and vowels, plus a couple of letters which have no sound of their own but which affect the sound of other letters). So the Russian script has got quite a lot in common with English! And remember – Russian really is much simpler once you know the script. Of course, if you are going to visit Russia, you need a basic recognition of the script, at least to be able to read the street signs and find your way around. The handwritten alphabet is a little different from the printed version – you will be meeting both forms in this book.

How the units work

There are ten units. In the first four units the printed alphabet will be introduced in manageable chunks of between five and 12 letters, which will be explained and practised. In these units each new Russian word will also be transliterated so that you can practise saying the words as well as reading and writing them. The fifth unit will concentrate on revision of everything covered in the first four units. In Units 6 and 7 you will learn how to read and write the handwritten Russian script; it is very useful to be able to recognize this (it is often used 'decoratively' in advertisements, for example) and it is actually much quicker to write using the script rather than copying printed letters. Finally, in Units 8 to 10 you will be given practice with words on specific topics, to give you a real sense of building vocabulary, as well as reinforcing your knowledge of both alphabets.

Within the units you will find:

- a list of things you can expect to learn
- the symbol **i**, which introduces key facts about pronunciation, spelling and cultural information
- examples of words using the new letters
- exercises for you to practise your new knowledge (answers will be found in the Key)
- English transliterations of the Russian words and phrases

Two ways of helping yourself to feel at home with Russian script

- In the first four units you may be asked to cover up the transliterated versions of Russian words in a right-hand column so that you can check that you really do recognize the letters in the Russian words in the left-hand column.
- Always practise saying the words out loud as you meet them (one of the straightforward things about Russian is that it is usually pronounced exactly as it is written) – by making the sound of each individual letter, you get the sound of the whole word, which makes it a lot easier than English with its complicated spellings (e.g. *bough* but en*ough*).

01

the printed alphabet (1)

In this unit you will learn to recognize
- two vowels
- three consonants

You will find these letters reassuringly familiar, as they look and sound very much like their English counterparts. Remember that the most important thing in this unit is to learn to recognize and read the five letters (don't worry at this stage about learning vocabulary).

New letters: two vowels

The first vowel

small	a
capital	A

This is pronounced like *a* in f*a*ther.

Just by learning this letter you already know how to say several different things, because, in Russian **a** means:

Letter	Meaning
a	*and*
a	*but*
a!	*ah!*
a?	*'I'll post it now, **shall I**?'* *'Ring me tomorrow, **would you**?'*

The second vowel

small	o
capital	O

This is pronounced like *o* in b*o*re.

This letter also has meanings of its own:

Letter	Meaning
o	*He's thinking **of/about** Moscow*
o	*I hit my hand **on/against** the wall*
o!	**Oh** *no!*

If we join the two vowels together, we get the initials which stand for *joint-stock company* (a bit like the English *plc*): **AO**.

New letters: three consonants

The first consonant

small	к
capital	K

This is pronounced like *k* in *k*ite.

We can use the vowel **a** with this letter to make a very common word:

Letter	Russian word	Meaning
к	как	*how* (as in '*How are you?*') *as* (as in '*I did as you asked*') *what!* (as in '*What?! Forgotten again?!*')

Remember that by making the sound of each individual letter, you get the sound of the whole word. So try that now: к + a + к = как.

The second consonant

small	м
capital	М

This is pronounced like *m* in *m*otor.

We can use the vowel **a** with this letter to make a word (although it's rather less common than как!):

Letter	Russian word	Meaning
м	мак	*poppy*

Remember that by making the sound of each individual letter, you get the sound of the whole word. So try that now: м + a + к = мак.

The third consonant

small	т
capital	Т

This is pronounced like *t* in *t*ired.

We can use the vowel **a** with this letter to make two very common words:

Letter	Russian word	Meaning
т	так	*so, thus*
т	там	*there*

Remember that by making the sound of each individual letter, you get the sound of the whole word. So try that now: т + a + к = так; т + a + м = там.

i So far we have met words of one syllable. If a Russian word has more than one syllable, it is important to know which syllable to 'stress' – i.e. which syllable to emphasize clearly. For example, in the Russian word for *mummy* there are two syllables. Look in the table to see which one to stress. The accent on the Russian word shows you that the first syllable is the one to emphasize (this is represented in the 'sound' column by the vowel in **bold** and underlined):

Russian word	Sound	Meaning
ма́ма	m**a**ma	*mummy*

The good news is that you never need to write the stress mark in – it's just there to help you, while you are learning. Of course, Russian isn't the only language where emphasis is important. In English, emphasizing the wrong part of the word can sometimes change the meaning (think of *record* and *record*), and there are very many words where it would sound decidedly odd if we emphasized each syllable equally (think how we emphasize the first syllable of *ever*, *everything* and *father* and 'throw away' the second or the second and third). This is what happens in Russian: pronounce the stressed syllable clearly and deliberately, but skim over the others, underplay them – don't give them any emphasis (much as we deal with the last syllable, for example, the -er of *ever*). Try this with the Russian word for *attack*:

Russian word	Sound	Meaning
ата́ка	at**a**ka	*attack*

The stress mark is perhaps most important when we are dealing with words which feature the letter **o**. If the **o** is in a word of only one syllable, then it will be pronounced as described above, like *o* in bore:

Russian word	Sound	Meaning
КОТ	kot	*cat*

If a word has more than one syllable and it contains an *o* which is stressed, it will always be pronounced like the *o* in bore. If, however, you see a word with more than one syllable which contains an *o* without a stress mark, 'throw it away' – pronounce it like the *a* in the English word *sofa*. Practise the words in the table, which gives you examples of stressed and unstressed *o*.

Russian word	Sound	Meaning
МОТÓК	mat<u>o</u>k	*skein* (e.g. of wool)
ÁТОМ	<u>a</u>tam	*atom*

Exercise 1.1

Over to you! Practise using the five letters we have just looked at by matching up the descriptions on the left with the Russian words on the right. Which goes with which? Say the Russian words out loud to help you work out the answers.

1 A physicist would be interested in this.   a ТАКТ
2 Someone allergic to cats would avoid this.   b ÁТОМ
3 A diplomat needs a lot of this!   c КАКÁО
4 A doctor would deal with one of these.   d КÓМА
5 You might drink this before you go to bed.   e КОТ

Exercise 1.2

You have already met all except one of the following words. Find the new word and you will also find out the name of a very large river which is particularly important in the Urals. All the words are in capitals, so there's no clue to help you!

1 КАК   4 МÁМА
2 ТАМ   5 КÁМА
3 КОТ   6 МАК

Exercise 1.3

Cover up the middle column and try reading the words in the left-hand column. How many did you get right first time?

Russian word	Sound	Meaning
АКТ	akt	*ceremony; formal document*
ÁТОМ	<u>a</u>tam	*atom*
КОТ	kot	*cat*
КТО	kto	*who*

Exercise 1.4

Now for a real conversation – even from just five letters! Can you work out what is being said?

Russian	Sound
A Кто там?	**A** Kto tam?
B Том, Мак.	**B** Tom, Mak.
A Как?! Том, Мак?!	**A** Kak?! Tom, Mak?!

1 What question are the two Scotsmen, Tom and Mac, being asked by A?
2 Is A surprised?

When you've checked your answers in the Key, try covering up the list on the right and practise saying the conversation on the left. (Did you spot that one Scotsman has a name which in Russian means *poppy*? – Which one? Yes, мак.).

Exercise 1.5

Choose the right word from the box (you might need to look back through the unit to track all these words down).

1 You want to find out *how* someone is.
2 You want to say that something is *there*.
3 You want to find out *who* is there.
4 You want to say that it is *so* hot.

как	кто
там	так

02

the printed alphabet (2)

In this unit you will
- meet two more vowels and five more consonants
- practise the letters learnt in Unit 1

The fun starts here! You will find the new letters reassuringly familiar to look at, but they sound rather different from their English look-alikes. By the end of the unit we'll already be over one third of the way through the Cyrillic alphabet.

New letters: two vowels

The first vowel

small	е
capital	E

This is pronounced like *ye* in *yet*.

If we combine this new vowel with some of the letters we learnt in Unit 1 we get the following words:

Letter	Russian word	Sound	Meaning
е	комéта	kam**ye**ta	*comet*
е	тéма	t**ye**ma	*theme*

The second vowel

small	у
capital	У

This is pronounced like *oo* in sh*oo*t.

Here it is in combination with other letters we have met:

Letter	Russian word	Sound	Meaning
у	аý!	a**oo**!	*Hey!* (calling for someone's attention)
у	тут	toot	*here*
у	ýтка	**oo**tka	*duck*

New letters: five consonants

The first consonant

small	в
capital	В

This is pronounced like *v* in *v*isit.

Here it is in combination with other letters we have met:

Letter	Russian word	Sound	Meaning
в	автома́т	avtam**at**	*automatic machine*
в	ва́куум*	v**a**koo-oom	*vacuum*

*Remember: pronounce each letter 'y'!

The second consonant

small	н
capital	Н

This is pronounced like *n* in *n*ovel.

Here it is in combination with other letters we have met:

Letter	Russian word	Sound	Meaning
н	моме́нт	mam**ye**nt	*moment*
н	нока́ут	nak**a**oot	*knockout*

Exercise 2.1

Over to you! Cover up the list on the right. The list on the left contains two common Russian first names, the name of an Austrian city and the river which flows through Saint Petersburg. What is the name of the river? When you've answered the question, have a look at the list on the right to check your reading of the script.

Russian	Sound
1 А́нна	**A**nna
2 Ве́на	V**ye**na
3 Нева́	Nyev**a**
4 Анто́н	Ant**o**n

The third consonant

small	р
capital	Р

This is the Russian letter 'r': it is rolled, pronounced like *r* in *r*at.

Here it is in combination with the other letters we have met:

Letter	Russian word	Sound	Meaning
р	тре́нер	tr**ye**nyer	*coach, trainer*
р	а́втор*	**a**vtar	*author*

*Remember that an unstressed **o** is pronounced like the *a* in sof*a*.)

Exercise 2.2

Over to you! These Russian words are all to do with sport. See if you can read them. Cover up the 'sound' column and the 'meaning' column until you have finished reading the word in Russian. Two of the words should look familiar – we've met them already in this unit.

Russian word	Sound	Meaning
карт	kart	*go-kart*
нока́ут	nak**a**oot	*knockout*
раке́тка	rak**ye**tka	*racket*
трек	tryek	*track*
тре́нер	tr**ye**nyer	*coach, trainer*

The fourth consonant

small	с
capital	С

This is pronounced like *s* in *s*ip.

Here it is in combination with other letters we have met:

Letter	Russian word	Sound	Meaning
с	Москва́*	Maskv**a**	*Moscow*
с	сестра́	syestr**a**	*sister*

*Another unstressed **o** in this word.

Exercise 2.3

Over to you! Here are the names of some Russian towns and rivers, but each one has a missing letter; the English version and pronunciation are given in the right-hand columns. Fill in the missing Russian letters.

Russian word	Sound	English version
1 Мý_манск	M**oo**rmansk	*Murmansk*
2 Н_вá	Nyev**a**	*Neva*
3 Омс_	Omsk	*Omsk*
4 Москв_	Maskv**a**	*Moscow*

Now write the missing letters in the order 1–4 and you will have the Russian word for 'river': **5** RIVER = _ _ _ _

The fifth consonant

small	x
capital	X

This is pronounced like *ch* in lo*ch* (in transliteration it is usually represented by *kh*).

Here it is in combination with other letters we have met:

Letter	Russian word	Sound	Meaning
x	крах	krakh	*collapse, crash* (financial)
x	харáктер	khar**a**ktyer	*character*

i More good news! In Russian there are no words for *a* or *the* (i.e. there are no indefinite or definite articles to learn), so, for example:

ресторáн   (ryestar**a**n)   means either *a restaurant* or *the restaurant*

трáктор   (tr**a**ktar)   means either *a tractor* or *the tractor*

Revision

We have already covered more than one third of the Cyrillic alphabet: four vowels and eight consonants.

Vowels	
a	like the *a* in f**a**ther
e	like *ye* in **ye**t
o	like *o* in b**o**re
y	like *oo* in sh**oo**t

Consonants	
в	like *v* in **v**isit
к	like *k* in **k**ite
м	like *m* in **m**otor
н	like *n* in **n**ovel
р	like *r* in **r**at
с	like *s* in **s**ip
т	like *t* in **t**ired
х	like *ch* in lo**ch**

12 down, 21 to go!

Exercise 2.4

Time to practise our 12 letters. Match up the Russian words in the first column with their English versions in the second column. Cover up the transliterations in the third column (unless you're really stuck).

1	ресторáн	a	*chaos*	1	ryestor<u>a</u>n
2	метрó	b	*toast*	2	myetr<u>o</u>
3	нос	c	*sauce*	3	nos
4	тéкст	d	*thermometer*	4	tyekst
5	тост	e	*restaurant*	5	tost

6 термо́метр	**f** *cosmonaut*	**6** tyerm**o**myetr
7 тон	**g** *nose*	**7** ton
8 ха́ос	**h** *metro*	**8** kh**a**-as
9 космона́вт	**i** *text*	**9** kasman**a**vt
10 со́ус	**j** *tone*	**10** s**o**-oos

Exercise 2.5

Look at the descriptions on the left, then try to fill in the missing letters in the middle column. Transliterations are given in the right-hand column – try not to look at it until you've had a go at all five questions!

1 A musician would play in one	ор_е́стр	ark**ye**str
2 An actor would act in one	теа́т_	ty**ea**tr
3 A fish would swim in one	р_ка́	ry**eka**
4 A waiter would work in one	ре_тора́н	ryestar**an**
5 A farmer would drive one	тра́к_ор	tr**a**ktar

Now write the missing letters in the order 1–5 and you will have the Russian word for *cross*:

6 CROSS = _ _ _ _ _

Exercise 2.6

You can compile five Russian words connected with music from the letters in the box. Can you find all five?

You should be able to find the Russian words for the following: note, orchestra, rock, tenor, tone.

а	е	к	н	о	р	с	т

03

the printed alphabet (3)

In this unit you will
- meet two more vowels and seven more consonants
- practise the twelve letters learnt in Units 1 and 2

The new letters in this unit may not look like English letters, but they do sound familiar to the English ear (and if you have studied Greek or mathematics you'll recognize some of them). By the end of this unit we will have covered almost two thirds of the Russian alphabet.

New letters: two vowels

These two vowels look very similar.

The first vowel

small	и
capital	И

This is pronounced like *ee* in f*ee*t.

Here it is in combination with some of the letters we met in Units 1 and 2:

Russian word	Sound	Meaning
вино́	vee**no**	*wine*
рис	rees	*rice*
такси́	taks**ee**	*taxi*
кино́	keen**o**	*cinema*

Exercise 3.1

Over to you! Practise using this new vowel along with the letters we have already learnt in Units 1 and 2. Here are some common Russian first names ... their transliterated versions are on the right, but they've been mixed up – sort out which goes with which:

1 Ива́н
2 Ири́на
3 Ки́ра
4 Ники́та

a K**ee**ra
b Neek**ee**ta
c Eev**a**n
d Eer**ee**na

When you've checked your answers in the Key, try covering up the list on the right and practise saying the names.

The second vowel

small	й
capital	Й

This is pronounced like *y* in boy.

This is called a 'short и' and 99% of the time you will find this letter following another vowel; it is used to make what in English is called a diphthong (two vowels pronounced as one syllable, like 'boy', 'Thailand'). It is occasionally found as the first letter of a word when Russian is trying to imitate the sound of a word from another language – e.g. it is required at the beginning of the Russian version of York: Йорк.

Here it is in combination with some of the letters we have already met in Units 1 and 2:

Russian word	Sound	Meaning
ай!	aiy!	*oh! ouch!*
Китáй	Keetaiy	*China*
май	maiy	*May* (the month)
райóн	raiyon	*region*

A very short, but much used, word in Russian is ой (oiy). It expresses surprise, pain, fear or rapture. So if you're expressing surprise because you've suddenly seen Ivan and you weren't expecting to, you might say:

Ой! Вот Ивáн!   Oiy! Vot Eevan!   *Oh! There's Ivan!*

Practise saying this, making sure you cover up the two right-hand columns.

New letters: seven consonants

The first consonant

small	б
capital	Б

This is pronounced like *b* in *b*ox.

The second consonant

small	г
capital	Г

This is pronounced like *g* in *g*oat.

Notice that it is a hard *g* (as in *g*et, *g*ive), never a soft *g* (as in the English *g*inger).

The third consonant

small	д
capital	Д

This is pronounced like *d* in *d*aughter.

Here are our two new vowels and our three new consonants from this unit in combination with some of the letters we have already met in Units 1 and 2:

Russian word	Sound	Meaning
банáн	ban**a**n	*banana*
табáк	tab**a**k	*tobacco*
гид	geed (hard 'g'!)	*guide* (a person who shows you round)
дóктор	d**o**ktar	*doctor*
агéнт	ag**ye**nt	*agent*
Мадрúд	Madr**ee**d	*Madrid*
Андрéй	Andr**ye**i	*Andrei* (a popular name for a man)

Exercise 3.2

Over to you! Practise our two new vowels and three new consonants – answer the following questions.

1 Russia's national drink is:
 a вóдка
 б вúски
 в винó

2 To withdraw money, go to the:
 a теáтр
 б дискотéка
 в банк

3 Which of these cities is not in England?
 a Бирмингáм
 б Гонкóнг
 в Йорк

4 Which of the following is a means of transport?
 a рáдио
 б áдрес
 в трамвáй

New letters: remaining four consonants

The fourth consonant

small	з
capital	З

This is pronounced like *z* in *z*oo.

The fifth consonant

small	л
capital	Л

This is pronounced like *l* in bott*l*e.

The sixth consonant

small	п
capital	П

This is pronounced like *p* in *p*each.

The seventh consonant

small	ф
capital	Ф

This is pronounced like *f* in *f*unny.

Here are our new consonants, з, л, п, and ф, in combination with some of the letters we met in Units 01 and 02:

Russian word	Sound	Meaning
зоопа́рк	zaap*a*rk	*zoo*
ана́лиз	an*a*leez	*analysis*
суп	soop	*soup*
па́спорт	p*a*spart	*passport*
факс	faks	*fax*
биле́т	beel*ye*t	*ticket*
фо́рвард	f*o*rvard	*forward* (e.g. in football)
профе́ссор	praf*ye*ssar	*professor*

Revision

We have now covered two thirds of the Cyrillic alphabet – we have looked at six vowels and 15 consonants (21 down, 12 to go).

Remember to cover up the right-hand column to test yourself. How many letters can you recognize?

Vowels	
a	like the *a* in f*a*ther
e	like *ye* in *ye*t
и	like *ee* in f*ee*t
й	like *y* in bo*y*
o	like *o* in b*o*re
y	like *oo* in sh*oo*t

Consonants	
б	like *b* in *b*ank
в	like *v* in *v*isit
г	like *g* in *g*oat
д	like *d* in *d*aughter
з	like *z* in *z*oo
к	like *k* in *k*ite
л	like *l* in bott*l*e
м	like *m* in *m*otor
н	like *n* in *n*ovel
п	like *p* in *p*each
р	like *r* in *r*at
с	like *s* in *s*ip
т	like *t* in *t*ired
ф	like *f* in *f*unny
х	like *ch* in lo*ch*

21 down, 12 to go!

Exercise 3.3

In the left-hand column are some common Russian first names, but each one has a letter missing. Their transliterated version is given in the right-hand column. Fill in the missing Russian letter.

1	Бори_	*Boris* (m.)	(unstressed 'o') Bar**ee**s
2	К´_ра	*Kira* (f.)	K**ee**ra
3	Па́_ел	*Pavel* (m.)	P**a**vyel
4	Ва_и́м	*Vadim* (m.)	Vad**ee**m
5	А́нн_	*Anna* (f.)	**A**nna
6	Сер_е́й	*Sergei* (m.)	Syergy**e**i
7	Свет_а́на	*Svetlana* (f.)	Svetl**a**na
8	Влади́ми_	*Vladimir* (m.)	Vlad**ee**meer
9	Ели_аве́та	*Elizaveta* (f.)	Yeleezav**ye**ta
10	И_а́н	*Ivan* (m.)	Eev**a**n

Exercise 3.4

Find the sports by using the letters from the box to fill the blanks in each word (you can use letters more than once).

а	б	в	е
й	к	л	о
с	т	у	ф

1 б _ _ к _ _ бол
2 в _ л _ _ бол
3 _ у _ бол

Exercise 3.5

Look carefully at the drawing of Vladimir's head.

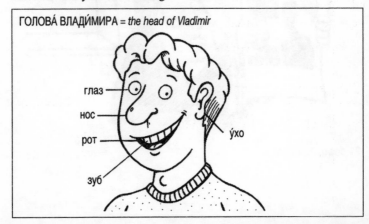

ГОЛОВА́ ВЛАДИ́МИРА = *the head of Vladimir*

глаз

нос

рот

зуб

у́хо

Vladimir isn't feeling well and he explains to the doctor what his symptoms are. The word болит (baleet) means *it hurts*, *it aches*, *it's painful*, *it's sore*. So when Vladimir wants to explain that his head aches, he says: болит голова (baleet galava).

What other symptoms is he complaining about?

	Russian	Sound
1	Ай! Болит ухо!	Aiy! Baleet ookha!
2	Ай! Болит зуб!	Aiy! Baleet zoob!

Exercise 3.6

Cover up the 'sound' and 'meaning' columns of each box and read the 'who/what' and 'place' words in the left-hand column. Then match up the 'who/what' words with the 'places' in the second box.

Who/what	Sound	Meaning
1 банкир	bankeer	*banker*
2 йогурт	iogurt	*yoghurt*
3 форвард	forvard	*forward*
4 опера	opyera	*opera*
5 тигр	teegr	*tiger*
6 флоппи-диск	floppee-deesk	*floppy disk*

Place	Sound	Meaning
a офис	ofees	*office*
b театр	tyeatr	*theatre*
c банк	bank	*bank*
d зоопарк	zaapark	*zoo*
e стадион	stadeeon	*stadium*
f ресторан	ryestaran	*restaurant*

For example: 1 → c: банкир → банк

Exercise 3.7

How many of these places can you recognize? This time, there's no right-hand column to help you (but you will find the answers in the Key).

1 Аме́рика
2 Аргенти́на
3 А́фрика
4 Ме́ксика
5 Кана́да
6 Кипр
7 Ку́ба
8 Пакиста́н
9 Уга́нда
10 Украи́на

04

the printed alphabet (4)

In this unit you will
- meet five more vowels, five more consonants and two 'signs' which have no sound of their own
- practise all the letters of the Cyrillic alphabet
- learn about Russian names

Most of the 12 new letters in this unit look very different from the characters of the English alphabet. They sound 'different' from English characters in the sense that more than one English letter may be needed to represent the sound of one Russian letter. We are going to meet five new vowels and five new consonants, plus two characters which have no sound of their own.

New letters: five new vowels

The first vowel

| small | ё |
| capital | Ё |

This does not look too unusual and is pronounced like *yo* in *yo*nder.

The second vowel

| small | ы |
| capital | Ы |

This does look unfamiliar. There is no real equivalent sound in English. With your mouth slightly open (but not moving your lips!), draw your tongue right back and say the English word *ill*. This letter sounds rather like the *i* of *i*ll if pronounced as described.

The third vowel

| small | э |
| capital | Э |

This may look backwards to you at first and is pronounced like *e* in l*e*t.

Exercise 4.1

Over to you! Practise saying these Russian words.

Russian	Sound	Meaning
её	ye**yo**	*her, hers*
всё	vsyo	*all, everything*
буты́лка	boot**i**lka	*bottle*
сын	sin (draw the tongue right back!)	*son*
экспе́рт	eksp**ye**rt	*expert*
экстрове́рт	ekstrav**ye**rt	*extrovert*

The fourth vowel

small	ю
capital	Ю

This is pronounced like *u* in *u*niversity.

The fifth vowel

small	я
capital	Я

Another letter which might appear to be backwards. This is pronounced like *ya* in *ya*rd.

Exercise 4.2

Over to you! Practise saying these Russian words.

Russian	Sound	Meaning
юрист	yur**ee**st	*lawyer*
юбка	**yu**bka	*skirt*
Ялта	**Ya**lta	*Yalta*
Италия	Eet**a**leeya	*Italy*

Exercise 4.3

Which of these countries is not in Europe?

	Russian	Sound
1	Испания	Eesp**a**neeya
2	Голландия	Gall**a**ndeeya
3	Япония	Yap**o**neeya
4	Германия	Gyerm**a**neeya
5	Англия	**A**ngleeya

Exercise 4.4

Now try your longest piece of reading so far! The only new word in this sentence is зовут (zav**oo**t) which means *they call*.

Russian	Sound	Meaning
Как её зовут?	Kak ye**yo** zav**oo**t?	*What is she called?*
		(literally, 'How her they call?')

Now choose the only appropriate name for her from the list in the middle column in order to complete the sentence which means *She is called...*:

	Possible names	Sound
Её зову́т _____	Серге́й	Syerg**yei**
	Ива́н	Eev**an**
	Ка́тя	K**a**tya
	Влади́мир	Vlad**ee**meer
	Бори́с	Bar**ee**s

New letters: five consonants

The first consonant

small	ж
capital	Ж

This is pronounced like *s* in plea*s*ure. (In transliteration it is usually represented by the English *zh*.)

The second consonant

small	ц
capital	Ц

This is pronounced like *ts* in ra*ts*.

The third consonant

small	ч
capital	Ч

This is pronounced like *ch* in *ch*eese.

Exercise 4.5

Over to you! Practise saying these Russian words.

Russian	Sound	Meaning
жасми́н	zhasm**ee**n	*jasmine*
жа́рко	zh**a**rka	*hot*
ци́ник	ts**ee**neek	*cynic*
цивилиза́ция	tseeveeleez**a**tseeya	*civilization*
чай	chaiy	*tea*
по́чта	p**o**chta	*post office*

New letters: two consonants

The fourth consonant

small	ш
capital	Ш

This is pronounced like *sh* in *sh*eep.

The fifth consonant

small	щ
capital	Щ

This looks very similar to the previous consonant, but note the extra 'tail'. It is pronounced like *shsh* in English *sh*ampoo.

Exercise 4.6

Over to you! Practise saying these Russian words.

Russian	Sound	Meaning
шарф	sharf	*scarf*
ша́хматы	sh<u>a</u>khmati	*chess*
щи	shshee	*cabbage soup*
ещё	yeshsh<u>yo</u>	*still, yet, more*

Exercise 4.7

Here are some leisure activities. Only one is musical – which is it? Remember to cover up the right-hand column – only look at it if you are stuck!

	Russian	Sound
1	виндсе́рфинг	veends<u>ye</u>rfeeng
2	джаз	dzhaz
3	пинг-по́нг	peeng-p<u>o</u>ng
4	ка́рты	k<u>a</u>rti
5	Скрэбл	Skrebl

Signs with no sounds

And finally – two characters which have no sound of their own, but which affect the way other letters are pronounced.

The 'hard sign'

| small ъ |
| capital Ъ |

The 'soft sign'

| small ь |
| capital Ь |

Neither of these letters occurs at the beginning of a word. The hard sign (ъ) occurs very rarely, is not pronounced and just makes a tiny pause between syllables:

Russian	Sound	Meaning
отъе́зд	at **ye**zd	*departure*

The soft sign, which looks very similar (ь), 'softens' the consonant which precedes it and is especially common after т and л. When pronouncing the soft sign after the Russian letter т, think of the way we pronounce the letter *t* in the English word s*t*ew (as if we're adding a soft, gentle *y* after the *t*). When pronouncing the Russian letter л with a soft sign, arch your tongue against your palate (i.e. not low in the mouth). In transliteration the soft sign is usually represented as follows:

Russian	Sound	Meaning
мать	mat'	*mother*
чиха́ть	cheekh**a**t'	*to sneeze*

УРА́! (oo**ra**! *Hurrah!*). We have now met all 33 characters – 11 vowels, 20 consonants and two characters (ъ, ь) with no sound of their own.

Exercise 4.8

Revise the alphabet! Check your knowledge of each letter in the tables.

Vowel	Sound	Russian	Sound	Meaning
А а	*a* in f*a*ther	банк	bank	*bank*
Е е	*ye* in *ye*t	ресторáн	ryestar**a**n	*restaurant*
Ё ё	*yo* in *yo*nder	её	ye**yo**	*her, hers*
И и	*ee* in f*ee*t	винó	veen**o**	*wine*
Й й	*y* in bo*y*	чай	chai**y**	*tea*
О о	*o* in b*o*re (when stressed; otherwise like *a* in sof*a*)	óфис	**o**fees	*office*
		áтом	**a**tam	*atom*
У у	*oo* in sh*oo*t	суп	soop	*soup*
ы	approximately like *i* in *i*ll	сын	sin	*son*
Э э	*e* in l*e*t	экспéрт	eksp**ye**rt	*expert*
Ю ю	*u* in *u*niversity	юрíст	yur**ee**st	*lawyer*
Я я	*ya* in *ya*rd	Итáлия	Eet**a**leeya	*Italy*

11 vowels done!

Consonant	Sound	Russian	Sound	Meaning
Б б	*b* in *b*ank	буты́лка	boot**i**lka	*bottle*
В в	*v* in *v*isit	во́дка	v**o**dka	*vodka*
Г г	*g* in *g*oat	гид	geed	*guide*
Д д	*d* in *d*aughter	дискоте́ка	deeskat**ye**ka	*discotheque*
Ж ж	*s* in plea*s*ure	жа́рко	zh**a**rka	*hot*
З з	*z* in *z*oo	зуб	zoob	*tooth*
К к	*k* in *k*ite	Кана́да	Kan**a**da	*Canada*
Л л	*l* in bott*l*e	литр	litr	*litre*
М м	*m* in *m*otor	метро́	myetr**o**	*metro*
Н н	*n* in *n*ovel	но́та	n**o**ta	*note* (music)
П п	*p* in *p*each	па́спорт	p**a**spart	*passport*
Р р	*r* in *r*at	ра́дио	r**a**dee-a	*radio*
С с	*s* in *s*ip	сестра́	syestr**a**	*sister*
Т т	*t* in *t*ired	тра́ктор	tr**a**ktar	*tractor*
Ф ф	*f* in *f*unny	факс	faks	*fax*
Х х	*ch* in lo*ch*	хара́ктер	khar**a**ktyer	*character*
Ц ц	*ts* in ra*ts*	ци́ник	ts**ee**neek	*cynic*
Ч ч	*ch* in *ch*eese	чай	chaiy	*tea*
Ш ш	*sh* in *sh*eep	шарф	sharf	*scarf*
Щ щ	*shsh* in English *sh*ampoo	щи	shshee	*cabbage soup*

20 consonants done!

Sign	Function	Russian word	Sound	Meaning
ъ	Hard sign – makes a tiny pause between syllables	отъéзд	at **ye**zd	*departure*
ь	Soft sign – adds a soft, gentle 'y' sound after a consonant	мать	mat' (think of how 't' is pronounced in 'stew')	*mother*

Congratulations! Now you have met all the printed characters of the Russian alphabet – the РУ́ССКИЙ АЛФАВИ́Т (r**oo**skeey alfav**ee**t).

Exercise 4.9

If you were a teetotaller, which of the following drinks would you order? The right-hand column is for emergencies only!

1 вино́   vee**no**
2 ви́ски   v**ee**skee
3 во́дка   v**o**dka
4 лимона́д   leeman**a**d
5 шампа́нское   shamp**a**nskaye

ℹ️ We have already met a range of common Russian first names. Now we are going to look at surnames and what are known as 'patronymics'. The patronymic is a middle name made up from the father's first name and the most polite form of address is to use someone's first name, followed by their patronymic (for example, you would address your teacher or your boss by their first name and patronymic). If you are a man, add -ович to your father's first name if it ends in a consonant, or -евич if it ends in -й (remove the й first).

First name	Patronymic	Surname	
Бори́с	Никола́евич	Помога́ев	is the father of →
Вади́м	Бори́сович	Помога́ев	

If you are a woman, add -овна (if your father's name ends in a consonant) or -евна (if it ends in й; but remove the й first) to your father's first name.

First name	Patronymic	Surname	
Борис	Николаевич	Помогаев	is the father of →
Татьяна	Борисовна	Помогаева	
Николай	Владимирович	Помогаев	is the father of →
Надежда	Николаевна	Помогаева	

Note that a woman's surname usually ends in -a or -ая, whereas a man's surname usually ends in a consonant or -ский.

Exercise 4.10

Look at the full names (surname – фамилия, patronymic – отчество and first name – имя) of the following two people:

1 фамилия: Кузнецова
  отчество: Валентиновна
  имя: Анна

2 фамилия: Горбунов
  отчество: Викторович
  имя: Андрей

1 What is the name of Anna's father?
2 What is the name of Andrei's father?

Exercise 4.11

Meet the Bykov family! First look at the Russian words for the members of the various generations.

Russian	Sound	Meaning
бабушка	ba**b**ooshka	*grandmother*
дедушка	d**ye**dooshka	*grandfather*
мать (мама)	mat' (m**a**ma)	*mother (mummy)*
отец (папа)	at**ye**ts (p**a**pa)	*father (daddy)*
сын	sin	*son*
дочь	doch'	*daughter*
дядя	d**ya**dya	*uncle*
тётя	t**yo**tya	*aunt*
внук	vnook	*grandson*
внучка	vn**oo**chka	*granddaughter*

Now look at the family tree below:

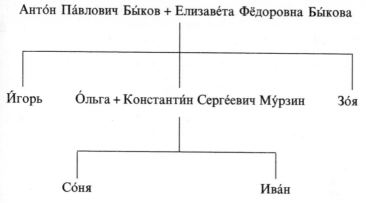

Now answer the following questions.

1 What relation is Ива́н Константи́нович Му́рзин to Анто́н Па́влович Бы́ков?
2 Two people will have the patronymic Анто́новна. What are their first names?
3 What is the patronymic of Со́ня?

Exercise 4.12

Look carefully at this advertisement for a concert and find the information to answer the following questions (a translation of the advertisement is given in the Key).

1 In which month is the concert taking place?
2 Which two composers are featured?
3 What is the name of the pianist?

Теа́тр о́перы и бале́та
КОНЦЕРТ

30 октября́ (в 12 часо́в)

Паганини

Конце́рт но́мер 1 для скри́пки с орке́стром

соли́ст Алекса́ндр Чирко́в

Рахма́нинов

Конце́рт но́мер 2 для фортепья́но с орке́стром

соли́ст Никола́й Байко́в

Exercise 4.13

All but one of the ten words in the table are connected with the world of finance. Find the odd one out (remember to cover up the right-hand column!).

Russian	Sound
банк	bank
креди́т	kryed**ee**t
креди́тная ка́рточка	kryed**ee**tnaya k**a**rtachka
инвести́ция	eenvyest**ee**tseeya
фина́нсовый кри́зис	feen**a**nsaviy kr**ee**zees
космона́вт	kasman**a**vt
до́ллары	d**o**llari
эконо́мика	ekan**o**meeka
капита́л	kapeet**a**l
банки́р	bank**ee**r

Check that you've understood the meaning of all the words by looking in the Key.

05

revision and reading practice

In this unit you will
- learn the proper order of the letters in the Cyrillic alphabet
- have lots of practice in reading words
- learn about months of the year and days of the week in Russian

The aim of this unit is to help you to consolidate your knowledge of the printed alphabet. In Unit 5 you'll have more practice in reading words and short phrases, but transliteration will not be given in Units 5–10. Learning the proper order of the alphabet is essential for later study if you need to use a dictionary or vocabulary list.

Russian has no present tense of the verb *to be* (*I am, you are*, etc.), so it's very easy to make statements in the present tense. Look at the following examples and note that when making statements of this kind, a dash is usually inserted (almost as if you were using the sign =):

Борис – инженер	*Boris (is an) engineer*
Светлана – медсестра	*Svetlana (is a) nurse* (literally, a 'medical sister')
Игорь – журналист	*Igor (is a) journalist*

Exercise 5.1

Look at the pictures on page 39 and decide which of the professions below fit which picture.

a футболист
b медсестра
c хоккеист
d инженер
e балерина
f журналист
g жокей
h пианист

Exercise 5.2

Look at the words **a–h** in the list above in Exercise 5.1. Did you understand them all? Check their meanings in the Key.

ℹ️ Asking questions is just as easy as making statements if you know the key words for asking questions. Here are four important ones:

где?	*where?*
как?	*how?*
когда?	*when?*
кто?	*who?*

And when we use them in questions:

Где Борис?	*Where (is) Boris?*
Как её зовут?	*What is she called?* (literally 'how her they call?')

1

2

3

4

| Кто Светла́на? | *Who (is) Svetlana? (the Russian way of saying 'what job does Svetlana do?')* |

| Когда́ матч? | *When (is the) match?* |

Exercise 5.3

You can answer the questions about Boris, Svetlana and the match by reading the following sentences. Complete the English answers that follow them:

Бори́с в суперма́ркете.
Светла́на – актри́са.
Матч в 21 час.

1 Boris is in the _____ .
2 Svetlana is an _____ .
3 The match is at _____ o'clock.

ℹ As well as making statements and asking questions, we can also easily contradict statements. Look at the following examples (parts of the verb *to be* are in brackets to remind you that the present tense of the verb does not exist in Russian):

| Нет! Бори́с не тенниси́ст, он боксёр. | *No! Boris (is) not (a) tennis player, he (is a) boxer.* |

| Нет! Она́ не медсестра́, она́ физиотерапе́вт. | *No! she (is) not (a) nurse, she (is a) physiotherapist.* |

| Нет! Чайко́вский не космона́вт, он компози́тор. | *No! Tchaikovsky (is) not (a) cosmonaut, he (is a) composer.* |

Exercise 5.4

Look at the examples above once more and then answer these questions:

1 What is the Russian word for *he*?
2 What is the Russian word for *she*?

Exercise 5.5

Look at the pictures below and then at the statements on page 41, which are incorrect. Complete the corrected versions which follow.

1 Виктор

2 Вадим

3 Александр

1 Виктор – журналист
2 Вадим – диск-жокей
3 Александр – гимнаст

1 Нет! Виктор не журналист, он _____ .
2 Нет! Вадим не диск-жокей, он _____ .
3 Нет! Александр не гимнаст, он _____ .

ℹ️ Most of the words we have met so far have been 'cognates', i.e. they sound very much like their English counterparts (see list A below). Of course, not all Russian words follow this pattern; although there are many which have a familiar sound, there are some which are more closely linked with Greek, Latin or with another modern European language (see list B) and others which sound nothing like their equivalents in English (see list C). Now look at the three lists of words. They are all connected with university life. You should find list A the easiest!

A

профе́ссор	*professor*
семина́р	*seminar*
студе́нт	*student*
университе́т	*university*

B

библиоте́ка	*library*
ка́федра	*university department*

C

иссле́дование	*research*
преподава́тель	*lecturer*

Exercise 5.6

Months of the year fall more or less into the 'A' group – i.e. their sound is recognizably similar to their English counterparts. Look at the months in the following list. Can you put them into calendar order? *January* has been done for you!

a	май		**g**	ию́ль
b	октя́брь		**h**	март
c	февра́ль		**i**	ноя́брь
d	ию́нь		**j**	сентя́брь
e	дека́брь		**k**	а́вгуст
f	янва́рь	= 1	**l**	апре́ль

i Days of the week, in total contrast, have very little connection with their English counterparts (although speakers of Italian and Spanish will recognize the word for *Saturday*):

Дни неде́ли *Days of the week*

Russian word	Meaning	Derivation
понеде́льник	*Monday*	*the Russian word for 'week'*
вто́рник	*Tuesday*	*the Russian word for 'second'*
среда́	*Wednesday*	*the Russian word for 'middle'*
четве́рг	*Thursday*	*the Russian word for 'four'*
пя́тница	*Friday*	*the Russian word for 'five'*
суббо́та	*Saturday*	*the word 'sabbath'*
воскресе́нье	*Sunday*	*the Russian word for 'resurrection'*

Exercise 5.7

Vladimir is a television addict who likes to plan his week's viewing in advance. Look at the list he has made, then answer the questions that follow:

Понеде́льник	10.10	Телесериа́л: Са́нта-Ба́рбара
Вто́рник	20.55	Кинофи́льм: Авиакатастро́фа
Среда́	21.35	Документа́льный фильм: Леге́нды теа́тра
Четве́рг	12.55	Ток-шо́у: Клуб футболи́стов
Пя́тница	15.45	Чемпиона́т: фо́рмула-1
Суббо́та	24.00	Гороско́п
Воскресе́нье	21.00	Коме́дия: Шо́у Бенни Хилла

On what day does Vladimir plan to watch:

1 a talk show?
2 motor racing?
3 a film about a plane crash?
4 a comedy show?
5 *Santa Barbara*?
6 a documentary film?
7 a horoscope programme?

Time to put all the characters we have learnt into alphabetical order. You have already met all the words given as examples, except:

| Евро́па | Europe |
| ёж | hedgehog |

А а	is for а́дрес
Б б	is for банк
В в	is for во́дка
Г г	is for гид
Д д	is for дискоте́ка
Е е	is for Евро́па
Ё ё	is for ёж
Ж ж	is for журнали́ст
З з	is for зоопа́рк
И и	is for инжене́р
Й й	is for Йорк
К к	is for клуб
Л л	is for лимона́д
М м	is for матч
Н н	is for ноя́брь
О о	is for о́фис
П п	is for па́спорт
Р р	is for ра́дио
С с	is for суп
Т т	is for такси́
У у	is for университе́т
Ф ф	is for факс
Х х	is for хоккеи́ст
Ц ц	is for цивилиза́ция
Ч ч	is for чай
Ш ш	is for шампа́нское
Щ щ	is for щи
ъ	No sound of its own and never used as the first letter of a word. See page 30.
ы	Never used as the first letter of a word. For pronunciation, see page 26.
ь	No sound of its own and never used as the first letter of a word. See page 30.
Э э	is for экспе́рт
Ю ю	is for юри́ст
Я я	is for Я́лта

Exercise 5.8

You are a tour guide and need to make an alphabetical list of the members of your group. Number 1 is indicated for you.

List of surnames	Position in alphabet
Кондратов	
Селезнев	
Носиков	
Бармина	1
Хоботова	
Лев	
Грязнова	
Вереев	
Туманова	
Давыдов	

How many members of the group are women?

Exercise 5.9

You are in charge of the small ads section in a newspaper office. Put the following advertisement sections into alphabetical order.

ТАЙМШЕР
КОМПЬЮТЕРЫ
АВТОЦЕНТР
БИЗНЕС
ТЕЛЕВИЗОРЫ
АНТИКВАРИАТ

Which section relates to:

1 cars?
2 antiques?
3 time share?
4 computers?
5 business?

Exercise 5.10

When you're looking at words which don't sound like their English equivalent, it's important to be able to find them in the dictionary or vocabulary list. Masha has made a list of the presents she intends to buy for birthdays this year. She is a very organized person and has put the names of her friends and family in alphabetical order on the left (overleaf). Using the vocabulary list to help you, answer the questions that follow:

Vocabulary list

велосипе́д	*bicycle*
духи́	*perfume*
кни́га по футбо́лу	*book on football*
конфе́ты	*sweets*
ча́йник	*teapot*
кулина́рная кни́га	*cookery book*
ми́шка	*teddy bear*
пла́тье	*dress*

Masha's list

Анна	←	духи
Бабушка	←	чайник
Вадим	←	велосипед
Валентин	←	мишка
Дедушка	←	конфеты
Константин	←	книга по футболу
Максим	←	кулинарная книга
Соня	←	платье

Who is going to receive:

1 a dress?
2 perfume?
3 a cookery book?
4 sweets?
5 a teapot?

Exercise 5.11

Look at the theatre ticket and use the vocabulary list to help you answer the questions which follow. (N.B. You do not need all the words on the ticket in order to answer the questions!)

Vocabulary list

вече́рние спекта́кли	*evening performances*
госуда́рственный	*state*
де́ти	*children*
до	*up to, until*
и́мени	*named after*
ме́сто	*place, seat*
нача́ло спекта́клей	*beginning of performances*
не допуска́ются	*not admitted*
парте́р	*stalls*
Пе́рмский	*belonging to Perm* (a city in the Urals)

пра́вая сторона́	*right-hand side*
ряд	*row*
цена́	*price*

1 After which composer is the theatre named?

Пермский государственный
театр оперы и балета имени П. И. Чайковского

ПТОБГ
№ 367

П А Р Т Е Р 30 MAP

ПРАВАЯ СТОРОНА

20 руб. Ряд 5   Место 9

Цена 4 р. 50 к.

Начало спектаклей в 19 часов. 30 минут.
Дети до 16 лет на вечерние спектакли не допускаются.

2 In which row will you be sitting?
3 Who are not allowed to attend evening performances?

Exercise 5.12

Which of the following words is *not* a subject which might be studied at school?

геогра́фия

хи́мия

фо́рмула-1

матема́тика

исто́рия

му́зыка

If you were to put this list of words into alphabetical order, which would come first and which would come last?

06
the cursive script (1)

In this unit you will
- meet the handwritten (or 'cursive') form of the first 16 letters of the alphabet
- learn more about Russian names
- learn some useful words for tourists visiting a Russian city

It is very useful to be able to recognize the handwritten script as it is often used for decorative effect in advertisements, on greetings cards, theatre programmes and so on, as well as in handwritten letters, notes etc. With one or two exceptions, the handwritten characters are not too strikingly different from their printed equivalents. Note that Russians would never write in the stress marks, so we haven't.

Handwritten characters

Here are the first 16 handwritten characters: compare them with their printed equivalents:

Printed capital	Handwritten capital	Printed small	Handwritten small
А	*А*	а	*а*
Б	*Б*	б	*б*
В	*В*	в	*в*
Г	*Г*	г	*г*
Д	*Д*	д	*g ∂*
Е	*Е*	е	*е*
Ё	*Ё*	ё	*ё*
Ж	*Ж*	ж	*ж*
З	*З*	з	*з*
И	*И*	и	*и*
Й	*Й*	й	*й*
К	*К*	к	*к*
Л	*Л*	л	*л*
М	*М*	м	*м*
Н	*Н*	н	*н*
О	*О*	о	*о*

Some of these need more getting used to than others.

The small version of г may look 'backwards' to you at first – it might help you to think of it as a backwards 's'.

Notice that there are two ways of handwriting the small letter д.

Full words

The real fun starts when full words are written. Notice particularly:

л   *л*

м   *м*

These must always begin with a little hook, so you cannot join them to a preceding о *о* .

Exercise 6.1

Practise your recognition of the first 16 handwritten letters: cover up the first (printed) column until you have tried to read the handwritten words. If you want to practise writing yourself, try writing the word in the third column and compare your results with the second column!

Printed word	Handwritten word	Your version	Meaning
Áвиа	*Авиа*		*airmail*
Банáн	*Банан*		*banana*
Винó	*Вино*		*wine*
Гол	*Гол*		*goal*
Да	*Да*		*yes*
Едá	*Еда*		*food*
Ёлка	*Ёлка*		*fir tree*
Женá	*Жена*		*wife*
Зóна	*Зона*		*zone*
Идеáл	*Идеал*		*ideal*
Йóга	*Йога*		*yoga*
Кинó	*Кино*		*cinema*
Лимóн	*Лимон*		*lemon*
Молокó	*Молоко*		*milk*
Нет	*Нет*		*no*
Одéжда	*Одежда*		*clothes*

Exercise 6.2

Which is the odd one out in the following list? Cover up the right-hand column unless you're really stuck.

Handwritten		Printed
1	*вино*	вино́
2	*водка*	во́дка
3	*лимонад*	лимона́д
4	*май*	май
5	*молоко*	молоко́

Exercise 6.3

Party time! Boris is making a list of friends to invite to his party. Match the handwritten Russian versions on the left with the English versions on the right.

1	*Елена*	a	Ivan
2	*Вадим*	b	Anna
3	*Иван*	c	Elena
4	*Анна*	d	Evgeny
5	*Евгений*	e	Vadim

ℹ️ All the first names above are the 'full' form. Russian makes considerable use of diminutive forms of first names, as an indication of affection or endearment. Here are some common Russian first names and their affectionate diminutive forms:

Full		Diminutive
Андре́й	→	Андрю́ша
А́нна	→	А́ня, А́ничка
Бори́с	→	Бо́ря
Влади́мир	→	Воло́дя, Во́ва
Еле́на	→	Ле́на, Ле́ночка
Ири́на	→	И́ра, И́рочка
Константи́н	→	Ко́стя
Никола́й	→	Ко́ля
О́льга	→	О́ля, О́ленька

These diminutive forms are used to address close friends, family and small children. The polite, formal way to address people is to use their first name and their patronymic, so if your boss is called

Константи́н Никола́евич Зелено́в, you will address him as Константи́н Никола́евич. If your son is called Константи́н, you would probably address him as Ко́стя (unless you're very cross with him!).

Exercise 6.4

More famous names! Who is the odd one out in this list of five famous Russians?

1 Че́хов
2 Толсто́й
3 Достое́вский
4 Рахма́нинов
5 Пу́шкин

ℹ️ The famous five include four of Russia's greatest writers and one composer. Practise reading their names in full. We start with the writer who was Russia's first truly great poet.

Name	Dates	One famous work
Алекса́ндр Серге́евич Пу́шкин	1799–1837	Евге́ний Оне́гин (novel in verse – *Eugene Onegin*)
Фёдор Миха́йлович Достое́вский	1821–81	Бра́тья Карама́зовы (novel – *The Brothers Karamazov*)
Лев Никола́евич Толсто́й	1828–1910	Война́ и мир (novel – *War and Peace*)
Анто́н Па́влович Че́хов	1860–1904	Дя́дя Ва́ня (play – *Uncle Vanya*)
Серге́й Васи́льевич Рахма́нинов	1873–1943	Конце́рт но́мер 2 для фортепья́но с орке́стром (Concerto no. 2 for piano and orchestra)

ℹ️ Russian grammar involves more changes to the endings of the words than we are used to in English (for example, nouns, adjectives and pronouns have 'case endings'). To understand extended sentences it is helpful to know how and why words change, but you can still work out meanings of short phrases without knowing the cases, as you will see in the next exercise.

Exercise 6.5

Look at the two extracts from advertisements and then answer the questions in English. (Look at the questions first!).

1 Which advertisement is from an estate agent and which from a travel agent?
2 What three buildings is the estate agent selling? What is claimed about the quality of these buildings?
3 Which countries are advertised by the travel agent? What activities are on offer in these countries?

Advertisement A

ТУРИНФО
АВСТРАЛИЯ –
виндсерфинг
серфинг
АВСТРИЯ –
автобусные туры
АФРИКА
*сафари в национальных
парках*

Advertisement B

АГЕНТСТВО-А1
ОФИС
ФИТНЕС-ЦЕНТР
ПАРКИНГ НА 50
АВТОМОБИЛЕЙ
класс А!!!!!

i If you are staying in Russia as a tourist or on business, there are a number of key words you will need to recognize. Some sound familiar.

ви́за	visa
гид	guide
па́спорт	passport
тури́зм	tourism
тури́ст	tourist
экску́рсия	excursion

Some key words are a little less obvious, although once you know their derivation they're easy to remember:

- When you arrive at your hotel you might be asked to fill in a БЛАНК (*form* – which is, of course, blank until you fill it in).
- If you stay in a hotel you are a guest – hence the word for *hotel* ГОСТИ́НИЦА, which comes from the Russian ГОСТЬ (*guest*).
- In a hotel your room will have a number – hence the word for *hotel room*, НО́МЕР, clearly a close relation of the English word *number*.

Exercise 6.6

Armed with the information just given, can you complete this КРОССВО́РД?

ПО ГОРИЗОНТА́ЛИ (Across)

1 Person who shows tourists round museum
2 You need this to enter other countries and return to your own
3 You need one of these documents in order to enter Russia
4 You need to buy one of these if you want to travel by train, plane or bus
5 Your hotel room

ПО ВЕРТИКА́ЛИ (Down)

1 A place where tourists stay
2 You might go here to see a play, opera or ballet

		¹		д		
		о				
²			п			т
	³					
	⁴	и			²	
					е	
	⁵	о				

When in Russia, it's important to understand the signs that tell you what's where.

банк	*bank*
вход	*entrance*
вы́ход	*exit*
перехо́д	*crossing* (or *subway*)
по́чта	*post office*
ста́нция метро́	*metro station*
у́лица	*street*

Be prepared for the endings of words to vary. Take care if you see this sign.

НЕТ ВХОДА!

Don't go in! The key here is HET *no*.

Exercise 6.7

In the left-hand column are some words you may come across in a Russian city. Match them up with their meanings in the right-hand column.

1	ка́сса	**a**	taxi rank
2	кио́ск	**b**	ticket office, cash desk
3	медпу́нкт	**c**	centre
4	мили́ция	**d**	kiosk
5	остано́вка авто́буса	**e**	telephone box
6	стоя́нка такси́	**f**	bus stop
7	телефо́н автома́т	**g**	police
8	центр	**h**	first aid

As a visitor to Russia you will also need to look out for this sign:

ОБМЕН ВАЛЮТЫ

This tells you where you can cash in your traveller's cheques or change money (in English, *foreign currency exchange*.)

Notice how close the second of these words, ВАЛЮ́ТА (*foreign currency*), is in sound to the English word *value*.

Exercise 6.8

Look at the list of foreign countries below. Can you work out what they are in English?

1 Норве́гия
2 Ита́лия
3 Кана́да
4 А́нглия
5 Финля́ндия
6 Голла́ндия
7 Украи́на
8 А́встрия
9 Фра́нция
10 Австра́лия

If you are a tourist travelling from a foreign country to Russia, you will need to change your money into roubles (рубли́), so you'll be interested to find out about the exchange rate: валю́тный курс.

Exercise 6.9

You have just arrived at your hotel in Moscow and are checking through the information leaflet in your room. Most of the words used are 'cognates' (sound roughly like their English equivalents), but there are three which don't:

врач *doctor*   услу́ги *service*   эта́ж *storey, floor*

Look at the information and answer the questions which follow.

АВИАБИЛЕТЫ	☎ 2549
БАНК	
1 этаж	
БАРЫ	☎ 2050
1, 2, 15 этажи	
БИЗНЕС-ЦЕНТР (факс,	
Электронная почта, Интернет)	☎ 2688
1 этаж	
БИЛЬЯРДНАЯ	☎ 2692
БУФЕТ	☎ 2031
1, 3, 5, 7, 9, 14 этажи	
ВРАЧ	☎ 2416
2 этаж	

ПОЧТА
  1 этаж
САУНА   ☎ 2488
СЕЙФЫ   ☎ 2458
СУВЕНИРЫ, Сувенирный киоск,
  2 этаж
ТАКСИ   ☎ 2091
ТЕАТРАЛЬНЫЕ БИЛЕТЫ   ☎ 2027
ЭКСКУРСИИ   ☎ 2027

Which number would you ring if you wanted to:

1 Visit the sauna?
2 Enquire about plane tickets?
3 Book tickets for the theatre?

Which floor would you need to go to if you wanted to:

4 See the doctor?
5 Buy some souvenirs?
6 Send a fax?

ℹ In Russian hotels, the ground floor is first floor (so the English 1st floor in Russia is этáж 2).

Exercise 6.10

The following list contains the sorts of books that are bestsellers. The list shows their order of popularity (their РЕ́ЙТИНГ).

Бестсе́ллеры   Рейтинг

  1 Детекти́в
  2 Автобиогра́фия
  3 Ю́мор
  4 Биогра́фия
  5 Истори́ческий романти́зм

1 What five categories of book are listed?
2 Now put the five categories in alphabetical order.

07

the cursive script (2)

In this unit you will
- learn how to recognize the whole of the Cyrillic alphabet in cursive form
- learn about how addresses are written in Russian
- learn about greetings
- learn about seasons and weather in Russia

Handwritten characters

Here are the last 15 handwritten characters (and two signs). Compare them with their printed equivalents:

Printed capital	Handwritten capital	Printed small	Handwritten small
П	*П*	п	*n*
Р	*Р*	р	*р*
С	*С*	с	*с*
Т	*Т*	т	*m, т*
У	*У*	у	*у*
Ф	*Ф*	ф	*ф*
Х	*Х*	х	*х*
Ц	*Ц*	ц	*ц*
Ч	*Ч*	ч	*ч*
Ш	*Ш*	ш	*ш*
Щ	*Щ*	щ	*щ*
		ъ	*ъ*
		ы	*ы*
		ь	*ь*
Э	*Э*	э	*э*
Ю	*Ю*	ю	*ю*
Я	*Я*	я	*я*

Notice that there are two ways of handwriting the small letter т. When it is written as *m* it is sometimes written with a line above it (*m̄*). Similarly, a line can be used below the letter *ш* (*ш̱*). This makes them easier to distinguish from the letters they are joined on to.

Like the letters л and м, the letter *я* must always begin with a little hook, so you cannot join it to a preceding *о* .

Exercise 7.1

Practise your recognition of the last batch of handwritten letters: cover up the first (printed) column until you have tried to read the first handwritten word. If you want to practise writing yourself, try writing the word in the third column and compare your results with the second column.

Printed word	Handwritten word	Your version	Meaning
Почта	*Почта*		*post office*
Рестора́н	*Ресторан*		*restaurant*
Студе́нт	*Студент*		*student*
Тури́ст	*Турист*		*tourist*
Университе́т	*Университет*		*university*
Футбо́л	*Футбол*		*football*
Хокке́й	*Хоккей*		*hockey*
Центр	*Центр*		*centre*
Чай	*Чай*		*tea*
Ша́хматы	*Шахматы*		*chess*
Щи	*Щи*		*cabbage soup*
Отъе́зд*	*Отъезд*		*departure*
Вы*	*Вы*		*you* (polite form)
То́лько*	*Только*		*only*
Эта́ж	*Этаж*		*storey, floor*
Ю́бка	*Юбка*		*skirt*
Язы́к	*Язык*		*language, tongue*

*The letters ъ, ы, ь are never found at the beginning of a word.

Exercise 7.2

Which is the odd one out in the following list? Cover up the right-hand column unless you're really stuck.

Handwritten	Printed
1 *актёр*	актёр
2 *балет*	балéт
3 *опера*	óпера
4 *театр*	теáтр
5 *шахматы*	шáхматы

ℹ️ It is usual to write addresses in Russian in reverse order to the English address. The Russian system deals first of all with the 'where':

куда́ (literally, 'to where')

First comes the country, then the town and its code, then the street (with the number of the block of flats and the flat number), for example:

Росси́я	*Russia*
103786 Москва́	*103786 Moscow*
ул. Стаха́нова, дом 4, кв. 19	*Stakhanov Street, block 4, flat 19*

In this part of the address, ул. is an abbreviation for у́лица *street*, дом is *house* and кв. is an abbreviation for кварти́ра *flat*.

The final part of the address deals with the addressee:

кому́ *to whom*

There is often a third address section on the front of a Russian envelope. This is where you, as the sender, write your address. You will usually see the words а́дрес отправи́теля *address of sender* if this is the case.

Exercise 7.3

Look at the envelope overleaf, then answer the questions which follow.

Куда: *Россия*

716400 Екатеринбург
ул. Гагарина, д.58, кв.22

Кому: *Уткину. Б. П.*

Адрес отправителя:

814041 Владивосток
ул. Луначарского д.22 кв3
Кузнецов, А. В.

1 To which city is the letter being sent?
2 Where does the sender live?

ℹ️ Greetings cards are a popular way of celebrating festivals, just as they are in England. The most common greeting you will see on a card is one which will cover all occasions:

С пра́здником!	*Best wishes* (literally, 'with the celebration')

Other popular ones include:

С днём рожде́ния	*Happy Birthday!* (literally, 'with day of birth')
С Но́вым го́дом!	*Happy New Year!* (literally, 'with the new year')
Сча́стья в Но́вом году́!	*Happiness in the New Year!*

There are greetings cards, too, for Christmas (Orthodox Christmas is celebrated on January 7) and Easter. The greeting you are likely to see on a Christmas card is:

С Рождество́м!	(literally, 'with the Nativity')

or

С Рождество́м Христо́вым!	(literally, 'with the Nativity of Christ')

Easter cards are usually a bit more complex and include part or all of the Orthodox Easter greeting:

| Христо́с воскре́се! | Christ is risen! |
| Вои́стину воскре́се! | Christ is risen indeed! |

Now you can see very clearly where the Russian for 'Sunday' (воскресе́нье) has come from.

С днём рожде́ния *Happy Birthday!*

Exercise 7.4

On special occasions you might want to give flowers as a present. What are the flowers in the list below? There is a missing letter in each word – can you work out what it is?

1 на_ци́сс   daffodil (narcissus)
2 глади_лус   gladiolus
3 хри_анте́ма   chrysanthemum
4 при́мул_   primula

The missing letters spell the name of another flower. What is it? _ _ _ _

Exercise 7.5

Or you might want to give a useful book! Look at the advertisement below in which the company МИР РУССКОЙ КУЛЬТУРЫ (The World of Russian Culture) is advertising five new encyclopaedias.

What are the topics of these five encyclopaedias?

НОВАЯ СЕРИЯ!!

Популярная медицинская энциклопедия

Энциклопедия русской истории

Энциклопедия русской литературы

Энциклопедия русской музыки

Энциклопедия скандалов

Exercise 7.6

In Unit 5 we looked at months of the year. Six months of the year appear in the right-hand column. Select the appropriate month to match the occasions on the left:

1 Christmas in Russia   a окт́ябрь
2 Christmas in England   b сент́ябрь
3 Dostoevsky born 30 October 1821   c а́вгуст
4 Pushkin born 26 May 1799   d янва́рь
5 Tolstoy born 28 August 1828   e май
6 School year begins 1 September   f дека́брь

i The Russian words for the seasons bear very little resemblance to their English counterparts (although the first syllable of the English word *autumn* might help you when you're trying to remember the Russian word!).

весна́	*spring*
ле́то	*summer*
о́сень	*autumn*
зима́	*winter*

Exercise 7.7

Ivan's homework was to name two months for each season, but he has made some mistakes:

1 Which ones has he got right?

2 Sort the others out for him.

1 ВЕСНА
и́юль
а́вгуст

2 ЛЕТО
март
апре́ль

3 ОСЕНЬ
сентя́брь
октя́брь

4 ЗИМА
дека́брь
янва́рь

The illustration is Дед моро́з *Grandfather Frost*, a close relative of Father Christmas, except that Дед моро́з makes his visit on 31 December.

i In a country that spans eight time zones, the seasons vary considerably, so you need to know whether you'll be in the north, south, east or west. The Russian words for the points of the compass may not sound too familiar at first, but there are ways of helping yourself to remember them:

юг	*south*	(think of Yugoslavia – 'south Slav land')
восто́к	*east*	(think of Vladivostok in the easternmost part of the Russian Federation)
се́вер	*north*	(think of the 'severe' weather they have in the north of Russia)
за́пад	*west*	(this word comes from the idea of the sun setting, or literally, 'falling' in the west)

In Unit 6 we saw that the endings of Russian words sometimes change, but that this needn't put you off! Look at these next two sentences (and cover up the translation on the right until you've tried to work out the meaning for yourself):

Ло́ндон на ю́ге А́нглии	*London is in the south of England*
Арха́нгельск на се́вере России	*Arkhangelsk (Archangel) is in the north of Russia*

So, if you want to say *in the north* etc., you must use the word на in front of the word for *north*, then add the letter 'e' to the end of the word:

на се́вере	*in the north*

Exercise 7.8

Ivan's been struggling with his geography homework on English towns! The sentences on the left are Ivan's. Correct them by completing his teacher's sentences on the right:

ИВА́Н   УЧИ́ТЕЛЬ (*teacher*)

1 Ло́ндон на се́вере.   Нет, Ива́н, Ло́ндон на ___
2 Бри́столь на восто́ке.   Нет, Ива́н, Бри́столь на ___
3 Йорк на ю́ге.   Нет, Ива́н, Йорк на ___
4 Ньюка́сл на за́паде.   Нет, Ива́н, Ньюка́сл на ___
5 Ливерпу́ль на ю́ге.   Нет, Ива́н, Ливерпу́ль на ___

ℹ РУ́ССКИЙ КЛИ́МАТ (the Russian climate)

Although it does get very cold indeed in many parts of Russia in the winter (–30° and –40° centigrade are not uncommon in some areas) it would be wrong to think that it is always cold everywhere in Russia – temperatures of +40° centigrade can be reached in the summer, even in some parts of Siberia. So here are some key words to describe the weather:

жа́рко	*it is hot*
идёт дождь	*it is raining* (literally, 'walks the rain')
идёт снег	*it is snowing* (literally, 'walks the snow')
хо́лодно	*it is cold*

Exercise 7.9

Here are the Russian expressions for *north-east* etc. Can you work out what they all mean?

1 ю́го-за́пад
2 се́веро-за́пад
3 ю́го-восто́к
4 се́веро-восто́к

Exercise 7.10

Look at the map of Russia below.

Now complete the weather forecast below with the appropriate weather vocabulary:

На се́веро-восто́ке _____. На

_____ идёт дождь. На се́веро-за́паде

_____. На ю́го-за́паде

_____.

−30°C

Exercise 7.11

On page 62 of this unit we met the expression C пра́здником – *best wishes* (literally, 'with the celebration'). As well as meaning *celebration*, the word пра́здник also means *festival* or *holiday*.

In the announcement that follows details are given of a series of festivals and you will see two words for *festival*: пра́здник and фестива́ль. Once again, don't be put off if the endings of words change!

Праздник русского театра	26 августа
Праздник! Диско-бал (лазерное шоу)	5 сентября
Фестиваль русской музыки	15 сентября
Праздник русского спорта	22 сентября

Which date would you be interested in if you were keen on:

1 sport?
2 music?
3 theatre?
4 disco music?

08

го́род и тра́нспорт

town and transport

In this unit you will
- consolidate your knowledge of the Cyrillic alphabet
- learn some names of Russian cities
- meet vocabulary on the themes of 'town' and 'transport'

i The word го́род means both *town* and *city*. Го́род appears as part of the name of some Russian towns – e.g. Но́вгород in the north-west of Russia means literally *new town*, even though it is one of Russia's most ancient cities. Founded in the 9th century and known as the 'father' of Russian cities, it is famous for its ancient churches and 14th-century frescoes (фре́ски). An important part of ancient Russian cities was the kremlin (кремль – which means *fortress*). The walls of Moscow's кремль enclose not just buildings with political and administrative functions, but also some of Russia's most beautiful cathedrals, with their distinctive cupolas (ку́пола).

Exercise 8.1

Here is a list of major Russian cities. Put them in alphabetical order:

Омск
Екатеринбу́рг
Тверь
Новосиби́рск
Яку́тск
Москва́
Владивосто́к
Санкт-Петербу́рг
Пермь
Ирку́тск

ℹ️ Russian towns are characterized not only by their kremlins, cupolas and frescoes – the average Russian city is distinguished by its wide streets and high-rise buildings. The majority of Russians live in flats (кварти́ры – from the English word *quarters*). The circus (цирк) is highly regarded in Russia and some major cities have their own circus building (a big top would not be appropriate in Russia's climate!); ice-skating and ice-hockey also enjoy great popularity, so an indoor and/or outdoor ice-rink (като́к) is standard.

Exercise 8.2

Look at the list of 'town' vocabulary – buildings you might expect to see in a Russian town. A translation is given only for the words we have not met before. How many of our old friends can you recognize without looking in the Key?

1	банк	
2	бассе́йн	*swimming pool*
3	библиоте́ка	
4	больни́ца	*hospital*
5	гости́ница	
6	дискоте́ка	
7	като́к	
8	кинотеа́тр	*cinema*
9	магази́н	*shop*
10	музе́й	*museum*
11	па́мятник	*monument*
12	парк	*park*
13	по́чта	
14	рестора́н	
15	собо́р	*cathedral*
16	стадио́н	
17	теа́тр	
18	у́лица	
19	це́рковь	*church*
20	цирк	

ℹ️ Many buildings (especially theatres, factories, libraries, universities) are named after famous people. Whenever this is the case, you will see the word и́мени, which means *of the name*. So, for example:

Библиоте́ка и́мени Ле́нина	*The Lenin Library* (literally, the library of the name of Lenin)
Институ́т и́мени Пу́шкина	*The Pushkin Institute* (literally, the institute of the name of Pushkin)

Exercise 8.3

In the anniversary edition of a theatre programme (below), you will see that the theatre is named after Tchaikovsky:

1 In which two art forms does it specialize?
2 In which city is it situated?

125 ЛЕТ

ПЕРМСКИЙ
АКАДЕМИЧЕСКИЙ
ТЕАТР
ОПЕРЫ И БАЛЕТА
ИМЕНИ
П.И.Чайковского

ℹ️ As a tourist visiting a Russian city, you will be interested to know about the sights that you can visit. Apart from the very large museums such as the Armoury in Moscow, or the Hermitage in Saint Petersburg, you will also find smaller museums which have been created in the buildings formerly occupied by famous people (e.g. the flats or houses of writers such as Pushkin, Dostoevsky and Chekhov). Many churches are now 'working churches', although some, especially the larger cathedrals, still have museum status. Works of art can be admired in a gallery or an exhibition hall, and there are also many palaces to visit, particularly in and around Saint Petersburg. So, here is a useful vocabulary list for a cultural visit to a town:

выставочный зал	*exhibition hall*
галере́я	*gallery*
дворе́ц	*palace*
дом-музе́й	*house-museum* (i.e. museum housed in building where a famous person lived)
иску́сство	*art*
кварти́ра-музе́й	*flat-museum*
музе́й-собо́р	*museum-cathedral*
Оруже́йная пала́та	*Armoury*
Эрмита́ж	*Hermitage*

Exercise 8.4

Here are the details in English of two tourist groups; followed by details of two excursions in Moscow:

Group A

Interested mainly in art and architecture

Group B

Interested mainly in literature and music

Экскурсия А2702

9ч30 отъезд
10ч30 Большой Кремлёвский дворец
15ч30 Третьяковская галерея
18ч30 Лекция «Русское искусство»

Экскурсия А2902

14ч30 отъезд
15ч00 Музей-квартира А.П.Чехова
17ч00 Лекция «Русская литература»
19ч30 Опера «Евгений Онегин»

---

1 Which excursion is the appropriate one for group B?
2 Which museum visit is mentioned in Excursion A2902?
3 Where exactly in Moscow is the palace mentioned in Excursion A2702?
4 What activity is on offer at 19.30 in Excursion A2902?

Exercise 8.5

The nine words in the box indicate different buildings in a town:

супермáркет

клуб

парфюмéрия

медпýнкт

поликлѝника

кинотеáтр

больнѝца

магазѝн деликатéсов

теáтр

1 Which three buildings would you visit if you were making purchases?
2 Which three would you visit if you weren't feeling well?
3 Which three would you visit in your leisure time?

Exercise 8.6

Anna has written a postcard below to her friend about her holiday in Moscow. She is keen to recommend the city and mentions four things she has found interesting. What are they? (Don't worry about changes to the endings of words.)

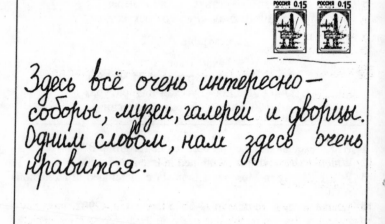

i Of course, you need to be able to get from A to B in a town, so it is important to know what sort of transport is available. Some of the major cities have an underground system, or metro, which is usually the preferred option (and also, in the case of Moscow, worth a visit to admire the distinctive decorations and sculpture of the stations). If you are travelling by metro, you will need to know where the station is, so you will find a plan of the metro helpful, or just look for a large M as you walk along the street. The Moscow metro has 138 stations and more than 90 kilometres of track; the first trains start to run at 5.30 a.m. and it closes at 1 a.m. Russian towns and cities also have buses, trams and trolleybuses. Depending on which city you are visiting, you may need a token or a ticket to travel on public transport. Otherwise, you can always travel by taxi.

Exercise 8.7

Here are the key words discussed in the paragraph you have just read. Can you work out what they all mean?

1 авто́бус
2 биле́т
3 жето́н
4 метро́
5 ста́нция
6 схе́ма метро́
7 такси́
8 трамва́й
9 тра́нспорт
10 тролле́йбус

i If you want to travel by bus, tram or trolleybus, look for a *stop*:

остано́вка

If you want to travel by metro, look for a *station*:

ста́нция

If you want to travel by taxi, look for a *taxi rank*:

стоя́нка такси́

Notice that all three words involve the letters с, т, and н – a good way to remember them is by thinking of the English verb *to stand* (which is what you are doing when you're waiting for your transport to arrive!)

If you're travelling further afield, the train (по́езд) or plane (самолёт) will be needed to cover Russia's vast distances. To catch a train, go to a *station*:

вокза́л

(Easy to remember because its derivation is the English word *Vauxhall*.)

The word for *airport* is easiest of all: аэропо́рт.

For most forms of transport the word по́ездка *journey* is used. This word is clearly a close relation of по́езд, but you can use it when you're talking about journeys by metro, bus, tram and trolleybus too.

Exercise 8.8

The metro ticket below is for two journeys:

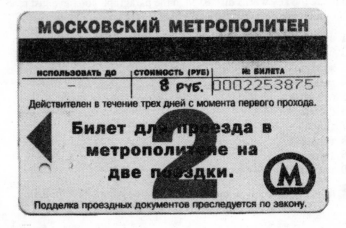

1 In which city can you use it?
2 How much did it cost?

Exercise 8.9

Here are the names of ten Moscow metro stations:

1 АЭРОПОРТ
2 БИБЛИОТЕКА ИМЕНИ ЛЕНИНА
3 БОТАНИЧЕСКИЙ САД
4 ИЗМАЙЛОВСКИЙ ПАРК
5 КИЕВСКАЯ

6 ПЛОЩАДЬ НОГИНА
7 ПУШКИНСКАЯ
8 ТРЕТЬЯКОВСКАЯ
9 УНИВЕРСИТЕТ
10 ЮГО-ЗАПАДНАЯ

1 Which metro station would you need to go to if you were staying at the Hotel Izmailovskaya?
2 Which station is named after a famous writer?
3 Which station would you go to in order to visit the south-western area of Moscow?
4 Which station would you go to if you were catching a plane?
5 Which station would you go to if you wanted to visit the Tretyakov Art Gallery?

As we have seen, some words relating to transport have clear western European origins – e.g. some of the public transport just mentioned (*bus, metro, taxi, tram, trolleybus*). We can see this too with some forms of private transport:

автомоби́ль or маши́на	*car*
велосипе́д	*bicycle* (the early English form of a bicycle was a 'velocipede' and the French word for 'bicycle' is *vélo*)
мотоци́кл	*motorbike*

Other 'transport' words are made up of Russian roots which explain what they do: самолёт *plane* literally means *self-flyer*, coming from the word сам *self* and the root of the verb *to fly*: лета́ть.

вертолёт *helicopter* is a *turning-flyer* (верт is a root meaning *turn*).

по́езд *train* comes from the verb *to go by transport*: е́здить.

Exercise 8.10

Which is the only Russian car in the box?

ЛАДА

МЕРСЕДЕС

ПАССАТ

РОУВЕР

ФОРД

ℹ️ Travelling by train across Russia can be a particularly interesting experience and is a good way to get to meet people, as well as to see the country. A journey to Perm (Пермь) in the Ural mountains, for example, takes approximately 24 hours from Moscow, travelling on the Trans-Siberian Express, which goes on for several days after the Perm passengers have alighted, (or by a 'local' train such as the Káma, which terminates in Perm and is named after the river which flows through that city). Siberia (Сибирь; in Tartar, 'the sleeping land') stretches from the Urals (Урáл) to the Pacific (Тихий океáн) – a distance of more than 3,000 miles. A ticket or 'travel document' (проезднóй докумéнт) for a long-distance journey will probably have the reference:

РЖД

This is the acronym for Russian Railways (literally, the 'Russian Iron Road' – рýсская желéзная дорóга). For a long-distance journey, check the number of your:

вагóн	*carriage*
купé	*compartment*
мéсто	*couchette/seat* (literally, place)

Exercise 8.11

Look at the travel document, then answer the questions that follow.

ПРОЕЗДНОЙ ДОКУМЕНТ		138465
АСУ «ЭКСПРЕСС»	РЖД	ЦЕНА 350 руб.
Поезд 22 МОСКВА – ПЕРМЬ 2		Отправление 25.03.03 19.00
Вагон 07		Прибытие 26.03.03 17.01
Место 05		

1 How much does the ticket cost?
2 What do you think the word Прибытие might mean?
3 Is 22 the number of the train, the carriage or the compartment?

Exercise 8.12 КРОССВÓРД!

ПО ГОРИЗОНТÁЛИ (Across)

1 An airborne vehicle with rotating blades
2 Where you do your shopping
3 The place to keep your money
4 A very large church
5 Sometimes you need one of these instead of a ticket
6 Entertainment involving animals and acrobats
7 An underground railway

ПО ВЕРТИКÁЛИ (Down)

1 Part of a train
2 The place to see plays, opera, ballet
3 A place where you can skate
4 You need to buy one of these in order to travel by bus, plane, train, tram or trolleybus

		1 в						2 т
2		г						
3 б	а		3		4		4 б	
			а					
	5	е						
6		к		7				

09

гостиница и ресторан
hotel and restaurant

In this unit you will
- have more practice in reading the Cyrillic alphabet
- learn how to count in Russian
- meet some useful vocabulary about hotels and restaurants

i Most tourists to Russia stay in the very large tourist hotels of the major cities, all booked in advance. These hotels tend to be named after cities, regions, countries, for example:

РОССИ́Я	*Rossiya* (means *Russia* – the large Moscow hotel near Red Square – КРА́СНАЯ ПЛО́ЩАДЬ)
ИЗМА́ЙЛОВСКАЯ	*Izmailovskaya* (a Moscow hotel situated just next to the metro station ИЗМА́ЙЛОВСКИЙ ПАРК)
МОСКВА́	*Moscow* (it's actually situated in Saint Petersburg!)
ПРИБАЛТИ́ЙСКАЯ	*Pribaltiyskaya* (one of the hotels used by visitors to Saint Petersburg and situated, as its name suggests, not too far from the Baltic Sea)

On arrival at your hotel you will register with the администра́тор (the *administrator*, at reception), who will ask you to leave your па́спорт and ви́за so that registration formalities can be completed. Most hotels issue visitors with a ка́рточка *little card* on registration – a useful document, which you often need to gain access to the hotel's main door and which is usually required by the lady on duty on each floor of the hotel before she hands over your key.

Exercise 9.1

Here is a list of 'hotel' vocabulary. A translation is given only for the words we have not met before. How many of our old friends can you recognize without looking in the Key (or Unit 6, where we first met them?)

1 администра́тор
2 бланк
3 ви́за
4 го́рничная   *maid*
5 гости́ница
6 дежу́рная   *lady on duty, responsible for floor of hotel*
7 ключ   *key*
8 но́мер
9 па́спорт
10 эта́ж

ℹ️ Russian tourist hotels tend to be very large and, as we saw in Unit 6, may have a whole range of facilities, from snack bars (буфéты) to a сáуна *sauna*. Here are some words we didn't meet in Unit 6:

бассéйн	*swimming pool*
казúно	*casino*
кéгельбан	*bowling alley*
кинотеáтр	*cinema*
лифт	*lift*
парикмáхерская	*hairdresser's*
ремóнт	*repairs*
стúрка	*laundry*
химчúстка	*dry cleaning*

РЕМÓНТ is a service, but it also means *repair*. You may see this sign in your hotel:

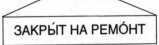

ЗАКРЫ́Т НА РЕМÓНТ

If you do, you will know that the facility in question is *closed for repair*.

Exercise 9.2

Look at the кáрточка.

САНКТ-ПЕТЕРБУРГ

ПЛОЩАДЬ АЛЕКСАНДРА НЕВСКОГО, 2

ГОСТИНИЦА МОСКВА

В центре города – Метро «Площадь Александра Невского»
тел 274 95 05

---

1 Why is this a very convenient hotel for the tourist?
2 What useful information does it give about how to get to the hotel?

We have met the word **пло́щадь** *square* twice:

Кра́сная пло́щадь	*Red Square*
Пло́щадь Алекса́ндра Не́вского	*Aleksandr Nevsky Square*

The original meaning of **Кра́сная пло́щадь** was *beautiful square* (so it has nothing to do with the red banners of Communism).

Пло́щадь Алекса́ндра Не́вского is named after Aleksandr Nevsky, renowned for his victory over the Swedes in the 13th century. The main street in Saint Petersburg is also named after him (**Не́вский проспе́кт**).

One of the services usually available in large hotels is foreign currency exchange. The key words in this context are:

обме́н	*exchange*
валю́та	*foreign currency* (Remember? It sounds like 'value')

If you are changing money in a hotel you will receive a record of your transaction, on which the cashier will indicate the sum exchanged and the amount of roubles received in words (not necessarily in figures). Russian numerals do not really bear much resemblance to their English counterparts, apart from **три** (*three*). *Ten* is **де́сять** and you can help yourself to remember this by thinking of *decimal*. Here are some of the Russian numerals:

1 оди́н	11 оди́ннадцать	30 три́дцать	400 четы́реста
2 два	12 двена́дцать	40 со́рок	500 пятьсо́т
3 три	13 трина́дцать	50 пятьдеся́т	600 шестьсо́т
4 четы́ре	14 четы́рнадцать	60 шестьдеся́т	700 семьсо́т
5 пять	15 пятна́дцать	70 се́мьдесят	800 восемьсо́т
6 шесть	16 шестна́дцать	80 во́семьдесят	900 девятьсо́т
7 семь	17 семна́дцать	90 девяно́сто	1,000 ты́сяча
8 во́семь	18 восемна́дцать	100 сто	
9 де́вять	19 девятна́дцать	200 две́сти	
10 де́сять	20 два́дцать	300 три́ста	

'Compound' numbers (e.g. 24, 55, 103) are easy in Russian – just place one number after the other:

24 два́дцать четы́ре
55 пятьдеся́т пять
103 сто три

Exercise 9.3

Here are some details from a currency exchange form at a bank in a Russian hotel. Look at it, then answer (in English) the questions below.

1 In which hotel is the exchange bank situated?
2 What is the client's surname?
3 Is the client resident in the hotel?
4 What sum of money is being exchanged?
5 How many roubles does the client receive?
6 What is the date of the transaction?

СПРАВКА БУ   ПУНКТ ОБМЕНА ВАЛЮТ 08908809
                       гостиница «РОССИЯ»
                       Москва
                       ул Варварка, д. 6

Клиент (фамилия)   Грант, М.

Резидент_____ Нерезидент_____✓_____

Сумма   двадцать долларов США

Получено клиентом   четыреста семьдесят рублей

23 марта 2003г

Exercise 9.4

While staying at the Hotel Rossiya in Moscow, Masha writes a letter to a friend and uses one of the hotel envelopes:

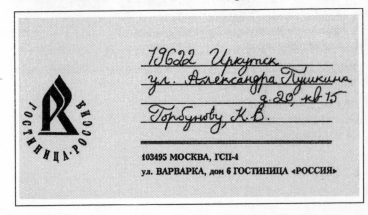

(handwritten address)

79622 Иркутск
ул. Александра Пушкина
д. 20, кв 15
Горбунову, К.В.

103495 МОСКВА, ГСП-4
ул. ВАРВАРКА, дом 6 ГОСТИНИЦА «РОССИЯ»

1 In which city does her friend live?
2 After which writer is the street named?
3 What is the number of the flat?

ℹ️ If you visit the hotel's буфе́т you are likely to have the choice of a selection of sandwiches and drinks:

бутербро́д	sandwich
во́дка	vodka
конья́к	cognac
ко́фе	coffee
минера́льная вода́	mineral water
чай	tea

A main meal in a restaurant, on the other hand, would be composed of a series of courses. First you'll want to consult the menu (меню́) and then place your order with the waiter (официа́нт) or the waitress (официа́нтка) – unless your set meals are part of a package. Starters (заку́ски) are a much more substantial course than in western Europe and might include salads, cold meats, smoked fish, small pasties and open sandwiches; this is followed by soup (суп), then a hot meat or fish course. The most usual desserts are fruit compote or ice cream. Bread (хлеб) is a very important component of any Russian meal and black (rye) bread is the most traditional: чёрный хлеб.

Exercise 9.5

The waiter in your restaurant is having trouble sorting out who has ordered what. You are with two friends who have ordered a light lunch and fortunately you jotted down what each of you chose. Here is your list:

Viktor:	soup, omelette, mineral water
Tanya:	salad, bread and wine
You:	soup, salad, bread, wine

Now here's what the waiter actually brings for you:

Ви́ктор	суп, сала́т, вино́
Та́ня	минера́льная вода́, омле́т, хлеб
Вы	суп, омле́т, вино́, хлеб

What mistakes has the waiter made?

i The three meals of the day are:

за́втрак	*breakfast* (in large hotels now often served on a self-service basis from a *Swedish table* – шве́дский стол)
обе́д	*lunch* (often the most substantial meal of the day)
у́жин	*supper*

Exercise 9.6

The excursion programme for the day is rather complicated:

08ч00	завтрак (гостиница Москва, ресторан А)
09ч00	отъезд
10ч30	Кремль и Красная площадь
12ч00	обед (гостиница Интурист, шведский стол)
14ч00	Исторический музей
18ч00	ужин (гостиница Россия, буфет этаж 15)
19ч30	Большой театр

1 Which meal will you be eating in the Hotel Rossiya?
2 Where exactly in the Hotel Intourist will you be eating?
3 What will you be visiting before lunch?
4 Where are you going after supper?

i Typical Russian foods are:

блин	*pancake*
икра́	*caviar*
квас	*kvass* (a drink made from fermented rye bread)
смета́на	*sour cream*

Soup is considered to be a hugely important part of the Russian diet; hot soups to give warmth in the cold of winter, but also cold, spicy soups in the intense heat of a southern Russian summer. The most well known of the hot soups in the West are: борщ *beetroot soup* and щи *cabbage soup*, although mushroom борщ with prunes can also be served cold. Other Russian soups include соля́нка (a spicy meat and vegetable soup with dill-pickled cucumbers) and окро́шка (a cold soup based on *kvass* or cider).

Exercise 9.7

Guests at a Saint Petersburg hotel have been asked to fill in a questionnaire about the hotel's services. They have been asked to give their assessment under three categories:

отлично	*excellent*
хорошо	*OK*
плохо	*bad*

They are assessing the standard of СЛУЖБА *service*. Look at the form of one guest, then answer the questions which follow:

	ОТЛИЧНО	ХОРОШО	ПЛОХО
служба приёма (администратор)			✓
служба этажа (дежурная)		✓	
рестораны	✓		
буфеты и кафетерии	✓		
бары	✓		
ремонт, стирка, химчистка		✓	
Дата заполнения: 19 ноября 2003			

1 Which is the only form of service the guest found to be poor?
2 Which things were found to be excellent?
3 When did the guest complete this form?

Exercise 9.8

You have just received a postcard from your Russian friend, who is on holiday in Saint Petersburg. Look for the key words to answer the following questions (you might need to revise some of the weather vocabulary in Unit 7).

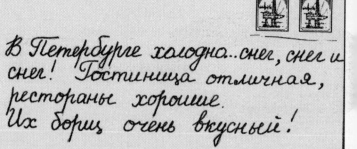

В Петербурге холодна...снег, снег и снег! Гостиница отличная, рестораны хорошие.
Их борщ очень вкусный!

1 What is the weather like?
2 What is the hotel like?
3 What food does she mention?

10

хобби
hobbies

In this unit you will
- revise all the letters of the
  Cyrillic alphabet
- meet some useful
  vocabulary about sport
  and other hobbies

Part 1 (Часть пе́рвая)

i Спорт enjoys great popularity in Russia. Some of the more popular forms of sport are related to the country's climate, for example:

КАТА́НИЕ НА ЛЫ́ЖАХ	*skiing*
ФИГУ́РНОЕ КАТА́НИЕ	*figure skating*
ХОККЕ́Й (НА ЛЬДУ)	*hockey (on ice)*

In fact, when you're talking about hockey in Russia, ice-hockey will be assumed. Another favourite in Russia is fishing (ры́бная ло́вля), and in the depths of winter you will see fishermen sitting by holes they have drilled in the thick ice of frozen rivers. Swimmers, too, are undaunted by the rigours of winter – in Moscow there are about 3,500 *walruses* (моржи́), intrepid swimmers who dig out areas in the ice so that they can swim outdoors all year round. Currently, their oldest member is 82 and their favourite air temperature for swimming (пла́вание) is –20° centigrade. The water temperature is apparently significantly warmer (especially near the river bed), but the walruses still emerge with icicles in their hair.

Exercise 10.1

Only one of the sports listed does not involve water. Which is it?

1 се́рфинг
2 пла́вание
3 виндсе́рфинг
4 баскетбо́л
5 ры́бная ло́вля

i A key verb involved with sport is 'to play': Игра́ть. The words linked to this (*game*, *play*, *player*) are easy to recognize because they all clearly have the same 'root' (i.e. they all start with игр):

игра́	*game, play (performance)*
игра́ть	*to play*
игро́к	*player*

When you're learning vocabulary, sometimes you can learn 'two words for the price of one'; so, in the case of this last group above, there are second meanings:

игра́ть	*to gamble*
игро́к	*gambler*

This kind of 'family grouping' of vocabulary is very common in Russian, so if you don't recognize a new word, it's always worth trying to work out what it means by looking for a root. In sporting vocabulary the groups work in very much the same way:

футбол	football
футболист	footballer
футбольный матч	football match
хоккей	hockey
хоккеист	hockey player
хоккейный матч	hockey match

The *football* root also provides us with the Russian word for a T-shirt: футболка.

Not all words associated with sport are so easily recognizable; although some you might be able to recognize by association, e.g. альпинизм (*mountaineering* – think of the Alps), but others are really not very obvious:

борьба	*wrestling*
гонки	*motor racing*
плавание	*swimming*
прыжок в длину	*long jump*
фехтование	*fencing*

The word for a *fan* in Russian is болельщик, which comes from the Russian word for *to be ill* болеть – in other words being a fan indicates a degree of obsession with your team. You might want to watch your team (команда) live at the stadium (стадион) or in the comfort of your own home, on the television (по телевизору).

Exercise 10.2

Read this little paragraph about Sergei and answer the English questions which follow (don't worry if you don't understand all the words – you'll still be able to answer the questions):

Сергей – хоккеист. Он играет в хоккей на стадионе. Сергей играет в футбол по средам и по субботам. Сергей не играет в футбол, но он любит смотреть футбол по телевизору.

1 Which sport does Sergei play at the stadium?
2 On which days of the week does he play?
3 Which sport does he watch on television?

Exercise 10.3

Match the sports in the left-hand list with the people who play them in the right-hand list. Hunt for 'roots' to help you.

1	волейбо́л	А	гимна́ст
2	гольф	Б	плове́ц
3	пла́вание	В	фехтова́льщик
4	борьба́	Г	игро́к в гольф
5	гимна́стика	Д	го́нщик
6	прыжо́к в длину́	Е	боре́ц
7	альпини́зм	Ж	прыгу́н
8	фехтова́ние	З	волейболи́ст
9	кри́кет	И	альпини́ст
10	го́нки	К	игро́к в кри́кет

Exercise 10.4

Where would you be able to participate in all these various sports? Choose the appropriate word for each sport from the box.

1 Tennis
2 Figure skating
3 Football
4 Swimming
5 Volleyball

БАССЕ́ЙН

ТЕННИ́СНЫЙ КОРТ

ВОЛЕЙБО́ЛЬНАЯ ПЛОЩА́ДКА

КАТО́К

СТАДИО́Н

Notice the word площа́дка (*pitch, ground*; literally, *little square*), a close relation of the word for *square* (пло́щадь) which we met in Unit 9 (e.g. *Red Square* – Кра́сная Пло́щадь).

ℹ️ Sports programmes on television are also extremely popular, especially if it is a футбо́льный матч or a хокке́йный матч.

Popular names for teams (not just in Moscow) are Dynamo (Дина́мо), Torpedo (Торпе́до) and Spartak (Спарта́к).

Not all leisure activities are connected with sport. Look at this list of other leisure activities. How many can you recognize without looking at the list on the right?

кино́	*cinema*
компью́терные и́гры	*computer games*
му́зыка	*music*
теа́тр	*theatre*
телевизио́нные програ́ммы	*television programmes*
ша́хматы	*chess*

Not all leisure vocabulary is so user-friendly. The following are not at all like their English counterparts:

рисова́ние	*drawing, painting*
чте́ние	*reading*

The word for *chess* (ша́хматы) is initially not very recognizable, but once you realize it comes from *checkmate* you'll find it easy to remember.

The Russian words for some more recent pursuits are clearly based on their English counterparts (e.g. ка́ртинг – *go-karting*), while others are adopting new English forms (for example, a motorbike fan could now be called ба́йкер instead of мотоцикли́ст).

Exercise 10.5

The following list of words needs to be sorted out under three headings: **1** Musical/Dramatic; **2** Sport; **3** Other. Which words will go under which heading?

A Бале́т	**Е** Шекспи́р «Роме́о и Джулье́тта»
Б Ша́хматы	**Ж** Атле́тика
В Телесериа́л	**З** Чте́ние
Г Хокке́йный матч	**И** Орке́стр
Д О́пера	**К** Гол

Exercise 10.6

The two advertisements (A and Б) are not completed. The graphics still have to be added.

1 Which box will the artist put drawing 1 into?
2 And drawing 2?
3 Where is the activity in Box A to take place?
4 For which day of the week is the activity in Box Б scheduled?

1   **2**

А

ЧЕТВЕРГ 10 ДЕКАБРЯ

ЛЕКЦИЯ «Компьютер – друг или враг?»

(Университет, 17ч30)

Б

СУББОТА 19 ДЕКАБРЯ

ВЫСТАВКА «Лучшие телесериалы нашего века»

(Библиотека, 09ч00–18ч00)

Exercise 10.7

You have just received a postcard from your Russian friend, Igor, explaining the activities on offer on his holiday. Look for the key words in it which will help you to answer the following questions.

1 Which two sporting activities are on offer?
2 What can the 'non-sporty' do?
3 Which resort is Igor staying in?

> Здесь можно играть в гольф
> и в теннис, смотреть фильмы
> или телевизор!
> Я люблю Ялту!

Exercise 10.8

You have just received a card (overleaf) inviting you to a 60th anniversary concert at a music school.

1 In which city is the concert to take place?
2 After which composer is the school named?

60 *лет*

Средияя специальная
музыкальная школа-лицей
Санкт-Петербургской консерватории
имени Н.А. Римского-Корсакова

Exercise 10.9

Rimsky-Korsakov, one of Russia's most famous composers, was also
a leading teacher and conductor. Look at the information about him
in Russian. Can you identify the words for: composer, conductor,
symphonies and suites?

Никола́й Андре́евич Ри́мский-Ко́рсаков (1844–1908) –
компози́тор (о́перы, симфо́нии, сюи́ты) педаго́г, дирижёр.

Part 2 (Часть втора́я)

And now for some general practice!

Exercise 10.10

You are trying to decide which restaurant to eat at. Don't be put off that you don't know *all* the words in the three adverts – you can still find the information you need.

Рестора́н А

ПАТИО ПАСТА

Итальянская еда в центре Москвы. Открыт с 12 дня до 12 ночи.

Рестора́н Б

ДАНИЛОВСКИЙ

Традиционная русская кухня. Элегантная обстановка. Открыт до 11 вечера.

Рестора́н В

СЕВИЛЛИЯ

Испанский ресторан. Широкий выбор вин. Открыт до 5 утра.

---

1 Which restaurant specializes in traditional Russian dishes?
2 Which is offering Italian food?
3 Which one would you choose if you wanted Spanish food?
4 Which one recommends its fine wines?
5 Which one claims to have an elegant setting?
6 Which one has a central location?

Exercise 10.11

The following announcement explains the procedure for using credit cards. Here's some vocabulary to help you answer the questions.

и́ли	*or*
име́ть	*to possess*
на́до	*it is necessary*
принима́ются	*are accepted*

1 In which three places can a credit card be used?
2 What else must you present with your credit card in order to use it?

КРЕДИТНЫЕ КАРТОЧКИ

Кредитные карточки
принимаются в гостиницах,
ресторанах и казино. Надо
иметь паспорт или
идентификацию.

Exercise 10.12

Which of the following is not a form of transport? What is it?

1 самолёт
2 автóбус
3 байк
4 велосипéд
5 вертолёт
6 трамвáй
7 бóдибилдинг
8 метрó
9 пóезд
10 троллéйбус

Exercise 10.13

Look at the floor guide of a large department store, then answer the questions:

ЭТАЖ	ОТДЕЛ
1	Книги, журналы, газеты
2	Багаж – сумки, чемоданы
3	Телевизоры, магнитофоны, компьютерная техника
4	Кафе-ресторан, туалеты
5	Музыка – ноты, кассеты, CD
6	Мода, парфюмерия

1 On which floor could you get something to eat?
2 Which floor specializes in computer goods?
3 Which floor would you go to if you wanted something to read?
4 Where could you buy some perfume?
5 Where would you go to buy luggage?

Exercise 10.14

You're checking through receipts from the exchange bank. Try to make out the amount of money changed by each client. The amounts are written in words, so you might find it helpful to look back to Unit 09.

Клиéнт А

Сумма	сорок пять долларов США
Получено клиентом	восемьсот девяносто рублей
27 февраля 2003г	

Клиéнт Б

Сумма	двадцать английских фунтов стерлингов
Получено клиентом	триста семьдесят рублей
12 апреля 2003г	

Клиéнт В

Сумма	сто канадских долларов
Получено клиентом	семьсот двадцать рублей
22 июня 2003г	

Клиéнт Г

Сумма	сто евро
Получено клиентом	шестьсот рублей
7 августа 2003г	

1 Which client changed money in June?
2 What sort of currency did this client change?
3 How many roubles did Клиéнт Б receive?
4 What sort of currency did Клиéнт Г change?

Exercise 10.15 КРОССВÓРД!

This final crossword draws on your knowledge of the vocabulary and on some of the 'cultural background' you have learnt during the units.

ПО ГОРИЗОНТÁЛИ (Across)

1 The most famous one is in Moscow, but many cities have one (it means 'fortress')
2 Important to know which one your hotel room is on
3 A secretary works in one
4 The place to visit if you're interested in history
5 If you like go-karting you'll want one of these
6 The male version of sister
7 A musician plays in one
8 The country where people speak Russian

ПО ВЕРТИКÁЛИ (Down)

1 This festival takes place in January in Russia
2 Third month of the year
3 This person works in a restaurant
4 An essential part of the Russian diet
5 Person who writes books
6 A food very popular in China

Unit 1

1.1

1 b atom, **2 e** cat, **3 a** tact, **4 d** coma, **5 c** cocoa

1.2

5 KAMA

1.4

1 Who is there?   **2** Yes

1.5

1 как, **2** там, **3** кто, **4** так

Unit 2

2.1

Невá

2.3

1 р, **2** е, **3** к, **4** а, **5** рекá

2.4

1 e, 2 h, 3 g, 4 i, 5 b, 6 d, 7 j, 8 a, 9 f, 10 c

2.5

1 к, **2** р, **3** е, **4** с, **5** т, **6** крест

2.6

нот, оркестр, рок, тенор, тон

Unit 3

3.1
1 c, 2 d, 3 a, 4 b

3.2
1 **а** vodka, 2 **в** bank, 3 **б** Hong Kong, 4 **в** tram

3.3
1 с, 2 и, 3 в, 4 д, 5 а, 6 г, 7 л, 8 р, 9 з, 10 в

3.4
баскетбо́л , волейбо́л, футбо́л

3.5
1 Ouch! My ear aches!   2 Ouch! My tooth aches!

3.6
1 c, 2 f, 3 e, 4 b, 5 d, 6 a

3.7
1 America, 2 Argentina, 3 Africa, 4 Mexico, 5 Canada, 6 Cyprus 7 Cuba, 8 Pakistan, 9 Uganda, 10 Ukraine

Unit 4

4.3
Япо́ния (*Japan*)

4.4
Ка́тя

4.7
джаз (*jazz*; the other activities are *windsurfing, ping-pong, cards* and *Scrabble*)

4.9
лимона́д

4.10
1 Валенти́н, 2 Ви́ктор

4.11
1 grandson, 2 Ольга and Зоя, 3 Константи́новна

4.12
1 October, 2 Paganini and Rachmaninov, 3 Nikolai Baikov

And for a translation of the programme:

Theatre of opera and ballet
CONCERT
30 October (at 12 o'clock)

Paganini

Concerto No. 1 for violin and orchestra

Soloist Aleksander Chirkov

Rachmaninov

Concerto No. 2 for piano and orchestra

Soloist Nikolai Baikov

4.13

космона́вт (cosmonaut) is the odd one out.

Russian	Meaning
банк	*bank*
креди́т	*credit*
креди́тная ка́рточка	*credit card*
инвести́ция	*investment*
фина́нсовый кри́зис	*financial crisis*
космона́вт	*cosmonaut*
до́ллары	*dollars*
эконо́мика	*economics*
капита́л	*capital*
банки́р	*banker*

Unit 5

5.1

1 b, 2 g, 3 e, 4 a

5.2

a footballer, **b** nurse, **c** hockey player, **d** engineer, **e** ballerina, **f** journalist, **g** jockey, **h** pianist

5.3

1 supermarket, **2** actress, **3** 9 p.m. (21.00)

5.4

1 он, **2** она́

5.5

1 космона́вт, **2** хоккеи́ст, **3** пиани́ст

5.6

1 f, **2** c, **3** h, **4** l, **5** a, **6** d, **7** g, **8** k, **9** j, **10** b, **11** i, **12** e

5.7

1 Thursday, **2** Friday, **3** Tuesday, **4** Sunday, **5** Monday, **6** Wednesday, **7** Saturday

5.8

Correct alphabetical order is:

Бармина
Вереев
Грязнова
Давыдов
Кондратов
Лев
Носиков
Селезнев
Туманова
Хоботова

There are four women in the group – Бармина, Грязнова, Туманова, Хоботова

5.9

Correct alphabetical order is: АВТОЦЕНТР, АНТИКВАРИАТ, БИЗНЕС, КОМПЬЮТЕРЫ, ТАЙМШЕР, ТЕЛЕВИЗОРЫ.

1 АВТОЦЕНТР, **2** АНТИКВАРИАТ, **3** ТАЙМШЕР, **2** КОМПЬЮТЕРЫ, **5** БИЗНЕС

5.10

1 Соня, **2** Анна, **3** Максим, **4** дедушка, **5** бабушка

5.11

1 Tchaikovsky, **2** Row 5, **3** Children up to the age of 16

5.12

фо́рмула-1 is not a school subject. The first word in an alphabetical form of this list would be геогра́фия and the last would be хи́мия.

Unit 6

6.2

4 май (*May*)

6.3

1 c, 2 e, 3 a, 4 b, 5 d

6.4

4 Рахманинов (*Rachmaninov*) is a composer; all the others are writers.

6.5

1 A=travel agent; B=estate agent, **2** office, fitness centre, car park (for 50 cars); class A (1st class), **3** Australia (windsurfing and surfing), Austria (coach/bus tours), Africa (national park safaris)

6.6

		¹г	и	д		
		о				
²п	а	с	п	о	р	т
		т				
	³в	и	з	а		
		н				
	⁴б	и	л	е	²т	
		ц			е	
		а			а	
					т	
	⁵н	о	м	е	р	

6.7

1 b, 2 d, 3 h (literally, 'medical point'), **4 g** (literally, 'militia'), **5 f, 6 a, 7 e, 8 c**

6.8

1 Norway, **2** Italy, **3** Canada, **4** England, **5** Finland, **6** Holland, **7** Ukraine, **8** Austria, **9** France, **10** Australia

6.9

1 2488, **2** 2549, **3** 2027, **4** 2nd, **5** 2nd, **6** 1st

6.10

1 Crime, Autobiography, Humour, Biography, Historical romance, **2** Автобиогра́фия, Биогра́фия, Детекти́в, Истори́ческий романти́зм, Ю́мор

Unit 7

7.2

5, ша́хматы (*chess*)

7.3

1 Ekaterinburg, **2** Vladivostok

7.4

1 р, **2** о, **3** з, **4** а, The missing letters give the word ро́за (*rose*)

7.5

Popular medicine, Russian history, Russian literature, Russian music, scandals

7.6

1 d, **2** f, **3** a, **4** e, **5** c, **6** b

7.7

1 Autumn and winter are correct. **2** He has got the months under spring and summer the wrong way round. They should be:

1 ВЕСНА	**2** ЛЕТО
март	и́юль
апре́ль	а́вгуст

7.8

1 ю́ге, **2** за́паде, **3** се́вере, **4** восто́ке, **5** се́вере

7.9

1 south-west, **2** north-west, **3** south-east, **4** north-east

7.10

1 идёт снег, **2** ю́го-восто́ке, **3** хо́лодно, **4** жа́рко

7.11

1 22 September, **2** 15 September, **3** 26 August, **4** 5 September

Unit 8

8.1

Владивосто́к
Екатеринбу́рг
Ирку́тск
Москва́
Новосиби́рск
Омск
Пермь
Санкт-Петербу́рг
Тверь
Яку́тск

8.2

1 bank, **3** library, **5** hotel, **6** discotheque, **7** ice-rink, **8** кинотеа́тр is the building; кино́ is either the building or the film medium, **13** post office, **14** restaurant, **16** stadium, **17** theatre, **18** street, **20** circus

8.3

1 opera and ballet, **2** Perm (Пермь)

8.4

1 A2902, **2** Chekhov's flat, **3** Kremlin, **4** The opera *Evgeny Onegin*

8.5

(*Vocabulary only given for words we have not met before.*)

1 магази́н деликатéсов *delicatessen*; парфюмéрия *perfumery*; супермáркет *supermarket*, **2** больни́ца; медпýнкт *first-aid post;* literally, *medical point*; поликли́ника *clinic*, **3** кинотеáтр; клуб; теáтр

8.6

собо́ры, музеи, галереи и дворцы (*cathedrals, museums, galleries and palaces*)

8.7

1 bus, **2** ticket, **3** token, **4** metro, **5** station, **6** metro plan, **7** taxi, **8** tram, **9** transport, **10** trolleybus

8.8

1 Moscow, **2** 8 roubles (8 руб.)

8.9

1 ИЗМАЙЛОВСКИЙ ПАРК (4), 2 ПУШКИНСКАЯ (7),
3 ЮГО-ЗАПАДНАЯ (10), 4 АЭРОПОРТ (1),
5 ТРЕТЬЯКОВСКАЯ (8)

8.10

ЛАДА

8.11

1 350 roubles, 2 Arrival (because it is roughly 24 hours after the train has left Moscow and has arrived in Perm), 3 Train

8.12 Crossword

		1 в	е	р	т	о	л	ё	2 т
		а							е
2 м	а	г	а	з	и	н			а
		о							т
3 б	а	н	3 к		4 с	о	4 б	о	р
			а				и		
	5 ж	е	т	о	н		л		
			о				е		
6 ц	и	р	к			7 м	е	т	р	о

Unit 9

9.1

1 administrator (receptionist), 2 form, 3 visa, 5 hotel, 8 hotel room
9 passport, 10 floor/storey

9.2

1 It is central (В центре города), 2 Name of the metro station to use: «Площадь Александра Невского»

9.3

1 Rossiya,   2 Grant,   3 No,   4 $20 (США – *USA*),   5 470,
6 23 March 2003

9.4

1 Irkutsk, **2** Pushkin, **3** 15

9.5

Viktor has got salad and wine instead of omelette and mineral water; Tanya has got mineral water and omelette instead of salad and wine; You have got omelette instead of salad

9.6

1 Supper, **2** self-service restaurant, **3** Kremlin and Red Square, **4** Bolshoi Theatre

9.7

1 Reception (administration), **2** restaurant(s), bar(s), snack bar(s) and cafeteria(s), **3** 19 November 2003

9.8

1 Cold and snowing, **2** excellent, **3** borshsh

Unit 10

10.1

4 basketball

10.2

1 hockey, **2** Wednesdays and Saturdays, **3** football

10.3

1 З, **2** Г, **3** Б, **4** Е, **5** А, **6** Ж, **7** И, **8** В, **9** К, **10** Д

10.4

1 Tennis → ТЕННИ́СНЫЙ КОРТ
2 Figure skating → КАТО́К
3 Football → СТАДИО́Н
4 Swimming → БАССЕ́ЙН
5 Volleyball → ВОЛЕЙБО́ЛЬНАЯ ПЛОЩА́ДКА

10.5

1 А, Д, Е, И; **2** Г, Ж, К; **3** Б, В, З

10.6

1 Б, **2** А, **3** university, **4** Saturday

А

THURSDAY 10 DECEMBER

LECTURE: 'Computer – friend or enemy?'

(University, 5.30)

Б

SATURDAY 19 DECEMBER

EXHIBITION: 'The best television serials of our century'

(Library, 09.00–18.00)

10.7

1 Tennis and golf, **2** watch films or television, **3** Yalta

10.8

1 Saint Petersburg, **2** Rimsky-Korsakov

10.9

композитор (*composer*), дирижёр (*conductor*), симфóнии (*symphonies*), сюйты (*suites*). Педагóг means *teacher*

10.10

1 Б, **2** А, **3** В, **4** В, **5** Б, **6** А

10.11

1 hotels, restaurants and casino, **2** passport or identification

10.12

7 бóдибилдинг (*bodybuilding*) i.e. a sport, leisure activity. The others are:

1 plane, **2** bus, **3** motorbike, **4** bicycle, **5** helicopter, **6** tram, **8** metro, **9** train, **10** trolleybus

10.13

1 4th floor, **2** 3rd floor, **3** 1st floor, **4** 6th floor, **5** 2nd floor

10.14

1 Клиéнт В, **2** Canadian dollars, **3** 370, **4** Euros

10.15 Crossword

		¹К	¹Р	Е	²М	Л	Ь			
			О		А			³О		
²Э	Т	А	Ж		Р		³О	Ф	И	⁴С
			Д		Т			И		У
⁴М	У	З	Е	Й				Ц		П
			С					И		
⁵К	⁵А	Р	Т			⁶Б	Р	А	Т	
	В		В					Н		
	Т		⁷О	Р	К	Е	С	Т	⁶Р	
	О								И	
	⁸Р	О	С	С	И	Я			С	

appendix

The Appendix is designed to give you some extra practice at recognizing the characters using a vocabulary list to help you revise the sequence of the alphabet and also to give you some extra opportunities for revising items of vocabulary.

First, here is an exercise requiring you to find the 'odd word out' of a group of words. Use the vocabulary list to help you check that you remember the meaning of all the words in each group, then decide which is the odd one out.

A1 весна́ ле́то о́сень гита́ра

A2 бутербро́д а́дрес конфе́ты сыр

A3 глаз нос а́вгуст голова́

A4 го́род обе́д за́втрак у́жин

A5 омле́т теа́тр му́зыка о́пера

A6 о́фис мать сын дочь

A7 пла́вание парк те́ннис футбо́л

A8 вто́рник суббо́та четве́рг по́чта

A9 университе́т снег студе́нт профе́ссор

A10 блин хо́лодно жа́рко дождь

Now choose the right answer for the following situations:

A11 If you were a tourist interested in history, which of these places would you want to visit: **a** стоя́нка такси́ **b** музе́й **c** бассе́йн

A12 Where would a waiter be most likely to work?
a больни́ца **b** банк **c** рестора́н

A13 What would you have to buy if you wanted to go to the theatre?
a биле́т **b** бага́ж **c** чемода́н

A14   If you were a tourist, where would you want to stay?
   a цирк   **b** це́рковь   **c** гости́ница

A15   If you were hungry, which of the following would be appropriate?
   a хлеб   **b** шарф   **c** но́мер

Answers

A1	гита́ра
A2	а́дрес
A3	а́вгуст
A4	го́род
A5	омле́т
A6	о́фис
A7	парк
A8	по́чта
A9	снег
A10	блин
A11	**b**
A12	**c**
A13	**a**
A14	**c**
A15	**a**

vocabulary list

In the vocabulary list the abbreviation (м) indicates a word which is *masculine* and (ж) a word which is *feminine*.

а́вгуст *August*
авто́бус *bus*
автомоби́ль (м) *car*
администра́тор *administrator* (receptionist)
а́дрес *address*
апре́ль *April*
аэропо́рт *airport*

ба́бушка *grandmother*
бага́ж *luggage*
бале́т *ballet*
банк *bank*
банки́р *banker*
баскетбо́л *basketball*
бассе́йн *swimming pool*
библиоте́ка *library*
би́знес *business*
биле́т *ticket*
бланк *form*
блин *pancake*
больни́ца *hospital*
борщ *beetroot soup*
бутербро́д *sandwich*
буты́лка *bottle*
буфе́т *snack bar*

ваго́н *carriage*
велосипе́д *bicycle*

вертолёт *helicopter*
весна́ *spring*
ви́за *visa*
виндсёрфинг *windsurfing*
вино́ *wine*
вку́сный *delicious*
внук *grandson*
вну́чка *granddaughter*
во́дка *vodka*
вокза́л *railway station*
воскресе́нье *Sunday*
восто́к *east*
всё *all*
вто́рник *Tuesday*
вход *entrance*
вы *you*
вы́бор *choice*
вы́ставка *exhibition*
вы́ход *exit*

галере́я *gallery*
где *where*
геогра́фия *geography*
глаз *eye*
голова́ *head*
го́рничная *maid*
го́род *town*
гости́ница *hotel*
гость (м) *guest*

дворе́ц *palace*
де́душка *grandfather*
дежу́рная *lady on duty* (on each floor of hotel)
дека́брь (м) *December*
день (м) *day*
день рожде́ния *birthday*
де́ти *children*
дождь (м) *rain*
дом *house*
дочь (ж) *daughter*
духи́ *perfume*
дя́дя *uncle*

ещё *still, again, more*

жа́рко *hot*
жена́ *wife*
жето́н *token*
журнали́ст *journalist*

за́втрак *breakfast*
за́пад *west*
здесь *here*
зима́ *winter*
зуб *tooth*

игра́ *game*
игра́ть *to play*
игро́к *player*
икра́ *caviar*
и́ли *or*
име́ть *to have*
и́мя *name*
инжене́р *engineer*
интере́сно *interesting*
ию́ль (м) *July*
ию́нь (м) *June*

как *like, as, how*
ката́ние на лы́жах *skiing*
като́к *skating rink*
кварти́ра *flat*
квас *kvass* (drink made from fermented rye bread)

кино́ (кинотеа́тр) *cinema*
клие́нт *customer*
ключ *key*
кни́га *book*
когда́ *when*
компью́тер *computer*
конфе́ты *sweets*
коньа́к *brandy*
кот *cat*
ко́фе *coffee*
кто *who*
куда́ *where to*
купе́ *compartment* (on train)
ку́хня *kitchen, cuisine*

ле́то *summer*
лифт *lift*

магази́н *shop*
май *May*
март *March*
матч *match*
мать (ж) *mother*
маши́на *car, machine*
ме́сто *place, seat*
метро́ *metro, underground*
минера́льная вода́ *mineral water*
мо́да *fashion*
молоко́ *milk*
мотоци́кл *motorbike*
муж *husband*
музе́й *museum*
му́зыка *music*
мы *we*

на́до *it is necessary*
нам нра́вится *we like*
нача́ло *beginning*
но́мер *number, hotel room*
нос *nose*
ноя́брь (м) *November*

обе́д *lunch*
обме́н валю́ты *currency exchange*
обстано́вка *setting, situation*

одéжда *clothes*
однúм слóвом *in a word*
октя́брь (м) *October*
омлéт *omelette*
он *he, it* (for masculine words)
онá *she, it* (for feminine words)
онú *they*
онó *it* (for neuter words)
óпера *opera*
óсень (ж) *autumn*
остановка *(bus) stop*
отéц *father*
отлúчно *excellent*
отправлéние *departure*
отъéзд *departure*
óтчество *patronymic*
óфис *office*
óчень *very*

пáмятник *monument*
парк *park*
пáспорт *passport*
перехóд *crossing*
плáвание *swimming*
плáтье *dress*
плóхо *bad, badly*
плóщадь (ж) *square*
пóезд *train*
понедéльник *Monday*
пóчта *post office*
прáздник *festival, holiday, celebration*
прибы́тие *arrival*
приём *reception*
пя́тница *Friday*

ремóнт *repair*
ресторáн *restaurant*
рисовáние *drawing*
Рождествó *Christmas*
Росси́я *Russia*
рот *mouth*
ры́бная лóвля *fishing*

самолёт *plane*

céвер *north*
сéрфинг *surfing*
сестрá *sister*
слýжба *service*
сметáна *sour cream*
смотрéть *to watch, look at*
снег *snow*
собóр *cathedral*
средá *Wednesday*
стадиóн *stadium*
стáнция *station*
стоя́нка такси́ *taxi rank*
студéнт *student*
суббóта *Saturday*
сýмка *bag*
суп *soup*
сын *son*
сыр *cheese*

такси́ *taxi*
там *there*
теáтр *theatre*
тётя *aunt*
тóлько *only*
трамвáй *tram*
трáнспорт *transport*
троллéйбус *trolleybus*
тури́ст *tourist*
ты *you* (singular, familiar)

ýжин *supper*
ýлица *street*
университéт *university*
ýхо *ear*

фами́лия *surname*
феврáль (м) *February*
фигýрное катáние *figure skating*
футбóл *football*

хи́мия *chemistry*
хлеб *bread*
хоккéй на льдý *ice hockey*
хóлодно *cold*
хорошó *good, well*

цена́ *price*
центр *centre*
це́рковь *church*
цирк *circus*

чай *tea*
чемода́н *suitcase*
четве́рг *Thursday*
чте́ние *reading*

шарф *scarf*
ша́хматы *chess*

щи *cabbage soup*

экску́рсия *excursion*
эта́ж *floor, storey*

ю́бка *skirt*
юг *south*

я *I*
я люблю́ *I like/love*
язы́к *language, tongue*
янва́рь (м) *January*

Finally, here are details of books and websites to help you develop your command of the Russian language:

Books

The first of the four books below deals with language to approximately GCSE standard; the others take you to a more advanced level.

- *Teach Yourself Russian Grammar*
  Daphne West
  Hodder & Stoughton 2003

- *Teach Yourself Russian*
  Daphne West
  Hodder & Stoughton 2001

- *A Comprehensive Russian Grammar*
  Terence Wade
  Blackwell 1996

- *Tranzit*
  Daphne West and Michael Ransome
  Bramcote Press 1996

- *Kompas*
  Michael Ransome, Daphne West and Rachel Smith
  Bramcote Press 2002

Websites

The following are all 'megasites' with many links to web pages on a huge range of topics related to Russia:

- Reesweb http://www.ucis.pitt.edu/reesweb
- Sher's Russian Index http://www.websher.net
- Slavophilia http://www.slavophilia.net

teach yourself

russian
daphne west

This is a complete course in understanding, speaking and writing Russian. If you have never learnt Russian before, or if your Russian needs brushing up, *Teach Yourself Russian* will give you a thorough grounding in the basics and will take you onto a level where you can communicate with confidence. The course contains:

- graded units of dialogues, culture notes, grammar and exercises
- a step-by-step guide to the Russian alphabet and its pronunciation
- an extensive grammar summary
- a Russian–English vocabulary
- an English–Russian key phrases section

By the end of the course you'll be able to communicate effectively and appreciate the culture of Russian speakers.

russian language, life & culture

stephen webber/tatyana webber

- What is the mysterious Russian soul?
- Where can you find palm trees in Russia?
- How much has Russia changed since the end of Communist rule?
- What do Russia's human 'walruses' do during the winter months

This book answers these questions, and many more, in a concise and lively overview of Russia: the country, its heritage and its people. Vocabulary lists and 'Taking it Further' sections at the end of each unit give the student and the enthusiastic traveller the means to talk and write confidently about all aspects of Russian life.

The book looks at: government, arts, language, work, leisure, education, festivals, food – and much more besides! This is your key to understanding Russia's past, present and future, with plenty of suggestions for further study and background reading.